SCHOLASTIC

Instant Content Area Vocabulary Packets

Joan Novelli & Holly Grundon

New York • Toronto • London • Auckland • Sydney
Mexico City • New Delhi • Hong Kong • Buenos Aires

Teaching *Resources*

Edited by Immacula A. Rhodes

Cover design by Wendy Chan

Interior design by Joan Novelli and Holly Grundon

Interior illustrations by Teresa Anderko, Maxie Chambliss, Sue Dennen, Kate Flanagan,
Rusty Fletcher, Anne Kennedy, Mike Moran, and Patricia J. Wynne

Vocabulary Comics illustrations by Mike Moran with the exception of page 27 by Anne Kennedy and Kate Flanagan
and page 37 by Patricia J. Wynne and Mike Moran

ISBN: 978-0-545-23694-2

Contents

Science Vocabulary Packets

Social Studies Vocabulary Packets

Math Vocabulary Packets

Introduction

O rdinal… asteroid… omnivore… How do children learn words like these? Most children begin kindergarten with an impressive vocabulary of about 3,000 words. That number jumps to 40,000 for the average high-school student (Nagy & Herman, 1987; Cooper, Chard, & Kiger, 2006). There are clearly many more words to learn than can be taught in a classroom setting, and research shows, in fact, that most children acquire the majority of their vocabulary through incidental experiences, including conversations (especially with adults), books they read on their own, and books others read to them (Diamond & Gutlohn, 2006).

But research also indicates that word knowledge cannot be left to chance. Both specific words and word-learning strategies need to be taught through explicit instruction (National Reading Panel, 2001). This is especially true for the often difficult and abstract words that students encounter in the content areas. Children can master sight-word lists and decode fluently. But if they lack understanding of word meanings, comprehension suffers. Vocabulary, then, acts as a "bridge" between decoding and comprehension (Kamil & Hiebert, 2005). Not surprisingly, there is a strong relationship between size of a student's vocabulary and overall achievement.

Instant Content Area Vocabulary Packets provides support for vocabulary instruction across the content areas with 25 reproducible activity packets that teach key concept words. Whether you are teaching a science lesson about Life Cycles (page 25) or a math unit on Measurement (page 135), the packets in this book will help students develop the word knowledge they need for success with content area comprehension.

> Of the many benefits of having a large vocabulary, none is more valuable than the positive contribution that vocabulary size makes to reading comprehension.
>
> (Nagy, 2005; Diamond & Gutlohn, 2006)

How to Use the Vocabulary Packets

Each five-page packet features a sequential set of activities that provides practice with a core group of content area vocabulary words. You can use the packets in any order to support topics of study in the classroom. You might have students complete one page per day for a week, or do several pages in one day. An overview of the packet format follows.

Page 1: Words to Know invites students to analyze their level of knowledge for each of six target words. Word Alert! promotes essential word-learning strategies, such as with roots and affixes, spelling patterns, multiple meanings, and context clues.

Page 2: Although it is generally agreed that it is not useful to simply have children look up words in dictionaries and write definitions, research does support the use of dictionaries as an independent word-learning strategy (National Reading Panel, 2001). My Mini-Dictionary provides practice with dictionary skills through kid-friendly pronunciations and definitions. To promote retention, students draw or write a clue about each word meaning. (Note that pronunciations are not provided for American Symbols, page 101. Say these words with students and have them repeat the words with you.)

Page 3: Vocabulary Comics features the target words in an appealing format to motivate reading and promote use of contextual analysis. As students select words from the Word Bank to complete a comic-strip story, they actively engage in thinking about the word meanings and their use. (For a writing connection, see page 7.)

Page 4: Three short activities further focus attention on the target words. Students examine syllables to promote word analysis skills (Syllable Smarties) and hunt for word features such as spelling patterns and silent letters (Word Hound). Make a Connection encourages students to connect the vocabulary to background knowledge.

Page 5: The Crossword reinforces understanding of word meanings and supports spelling skills with a twist on the familiar puzzle format. Students can use My Mini-Dictionary and Vocabulary Comics, as needed, to answer the clues. Then, using the letters in the shaded shapes in each crossword, they decode the answer to a Fun Fact Puzzler that promotes word consciousness. For example, in the Fun Fact Puzzler on page 105, students discover the name for a very large number (*googol*).

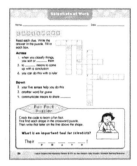

Tips for Teaching With the Vocabulary Packets

After selecting a vocabulary packet for students to complete, use the following model for guiding them in completing each page.

1. Introduce the words listed on page 1 (Words to Know). Invite students to share what they know about each word (for example, from previous encounters or by recognizing word parts). Then use the words in context and have students share what they think the words mean.

2. Walk students through the pages of each packet and review directions for completing each activity. Highlight learning goals for each activity.

3. Have students analyze their level of word knowledge by completing Words to Know (page 1 of each packet).

4. Then have students complete the remaining activities in order, beginning with Word Alert! (page 1).

5. As students work, look for opportunities to engage them in deepening their understandings of specific words. This might include saying the word together and noticing any special features (such as a familiar root), asking questions to elucidate meaning, talking about different uses of the word, and discussing word relationships.

Building Vocabulary With English Language Learners

To support English learners in working with the vocabulary packets, consider the following suggestions and strategies.

- Keep in mind that an English learner's background knowledge may not match the vocabulary packet topics. Fill in the gaps as needed to promote understanding.

- Be aware of letter-sound correspondences not in the student's native language, including as this relates to the target words in each packet.

- Use visuals, including pictures and graphic organizers, to help students make connections to new words.

- Teach cognates to help students use what they already know (August et al, 2005; Diamond & Gutlohn, 2006). For example, when using the packet for Our Government (page 65), point out to native Spanish speakers the cognates *democracy* and *democracia*.

Extension Activities

Support ongoing vocabulary development with the following activities, which provide further practice, invite exploration of word relationships, and nurture a playful approach to language.

Our Word Discoveries

Set up a Word Discoveries chart (see right) to record discoveries about word relationships, including synonyms, antonyms, homophones, multiple meanings, and figurative language.

Word Watch

Word	Synonyms	Antonyms	Homophones	Multiple Meanings	Figurative Language
volume				how much space something takes up; the degree of loudness; one book in a series (or one issue of a magazine or periodical)	
time			thyme		time flies when you're having fun; a whale of a time; in the nick of time

In *Bringing Words to Life: Robust Vocabulary Instruction* (Beck, McKeown, & Kucan, 2002), the authors stress the importance of noticing word use outside the classroom. To encourage this awareness in students, set up a Word Watch display that invites students to share "sightings" of words they are learning. Students can bring in the actual source of their sightings (such as a word used in a newspaper article), draw a picture (as in a word that appears on a sign), or simply write a note about where they encountered the word (as in a conversation).

Word Walls

Use the vocabulary packets to create word walls on each topic. Add to the word walls as students learn new, related vocabulary, then revisit them frequently to provide repeated encounters with the vocabulary. This is a good opportunity for word play, which fosters word consciousness and promotes life-long vocabulary learning.

Similar, Different Say a word that either has a similar or opposite meaning to one of the words on the word wall—for example, if the target word is *brook*, you might say *stream*. Have students identify the word and how it is related.

Mystery Word Provide clues to a word and have children guess what it is. Clues may relate to meaning or word features (such as number of syllables).

An Example of… Provide an example of the word and have students identify the word. For example, if the word is *urban*, you might name familiar cities.

Finish My Sentence Choose a word from the word wall and come up with a sentence that provides a clue to the meaning, but leaves out the word. Challenge students to complete the sentence. After a few rounds, let students take over and supply sentences for their classmates to complete.

Who, What, When, Where? Use questions to prompt critical thinking about words on the word wall, such as "Who would you find eating plants: a *carnivore* or an *herbivore*?"; "What would a measuring tape help you measure: *area* or *weight*?"; "When would you use *tally marks*: counting out money to buy a cookie or taking a survey about your classmates' favorite season?"; and "Where would you most likely to take a hike in the woods: in a *rural* area or an *urban* area?"

More Vocabulary Comics!

Page 3 of each packet features Vocabulary Comics, a comic-strip style story that uses the target words in context. Students can use the templates on pages 18–19 to create their own comic-strip stories using their vocabulary words. In addition to providing an appealing approach for practicing vocabulary words, this activity motivates and supports written expression. To use the speech bubble templates on page 19, students can cut around the basic shape of the speech bubble they want to use, then write text in the shape. They can also create their own comic strip formats on larger paper, and glue the speech bubble boxes inside each frame.

Connections to the Standards

Instant Content Area Vocabulary Packets provides support for meeting the following standards, as outlined by Mid-continent Research for Education and Learning (McREL), an organization that collects and synthesizes national and state curriculum standards—and proposes what teachers should provide for their students to become proficient in language arts, among other curriculum areas.

Reading

- Uses the general skills and strategies of the reading process (decoding, structural analysis, level-appropriate sight words and vocabulary, including from content areas)
- Uses viewing skills and strategies to understand and interpret visual media (as with main idea or message in visual media such as pictures and cartoons)

Science

- Understands Earth's composition and structure
- Understands the composition and structure of the universe and the Earth's place in it
- Understands the basic structure and function of cells and organisms and relationships among organisms and their physical environment (needs of plants and animals; life cycles; body systems; senses)
- Understands relationships among organisms and their physical environment (food chains; changes in the environment can be beneficial or detrimental and have different effects on different organisms)
- Understands biological evolution and diversity of life (some kinds of organisms that once lived on Earth have disappeared; there are similarities and differences in the appearance and behavior of plants and animals)
- Understands the sources and properties of energy
- Understands forces and motion
- Understands the nature of scientific knowledge and inquiry (how scientific investigations work)
- Understands the scientific enterprise (working with a team; science as an ongoing process)

Social Studies/Economics/Civics

- Understands concepts related to living and working together in families and communities, now and long ago
- Understands how democratic principles came to be and how they are exemplified by people, events, and symbols

- Understands the causes and nature of movements of large groups of people into and within the United States, now and long ago
- Understands concepts related to cultural contributions and national heritage
- Understands characteristics of different economic systems (buying and selling; goods and services; wants and needs; producers and consumers; supply and demand)
- Understands central ideas related to civics and American constitutional government (what a government does; how people work together; individual rights; how rules and laws solve problems)
- Understands the role of diversity in American life
- Understands the meaning of citizenship in the United States (rights and responsibilities; the importance of helping others; the way people influence decisions and actions by voting; the importance of leadership)

Math

- Uses a variety of strategies to problem-solve
- Understands and applies properties of number concepts
- Uses basic and advanced procedures while performing processes of computation (addition and subtraction; inverse relationships; multiplication and division; grouping)
- Understands and applies properties of the concepts of measurement (area, length, temperature, time, volume, weight)
- Understands and applies properties of the concepts of geometry (3-D shapes)
- Understands and applies basic and advanced concepts of statistics and data analysis (collecting, organizing, and displaying data; use of graphs)
- Understands and applies basic and advanced properties of functions and algebra
- Understands real-world connections in mathematics

Source: Kendall, J. S., & Marzano, R. J. (2004). *Content knowledge: A compendium of standards and benchmarks for K-12 education.* Aurora, CO: Mid-continent Research for Education and Learning. Online database: http://www.mcrel.org/standards-benchmarks.

Common Core State Standards

The activities in this book also correlate with the English Language Arts and Mathematics standards recommended by the Common Core State Standards Initiative, a state-led effort to establish a single set of clear educational standards whose aim is to provide students with a high-quality education. At the time this book went to press, these standards were still being finalized. To learn more, go to www.corestandards.org.

References & Resources

Archer, A. L., & Hughes, C. A. (2011). *Explicit instruction: Effective and efficient teaching.* New York: The Guilford Press.

Beck, I. L., McKeown, M. G., & Kucan, L. (2002). *Bringing words to life: Robust vocabulary instruction.* New York: The Guilford Press.

Biemiller, A. (2001). Teaching vocabulary: Early, direct, and sequential. *American Educator, 25*(1), 24–28. Retrieved from http://www.aft.org./newspubs/periodicals.

Block, C. C., & Mangieri, J. N. (2006). *The vocabulary-enriched classroom: Practices for improving the reading performance of all students in grades 3 and up.* New York: Scholastic.

Carnine, D. W., Silbert, J., Kame'enui, E. J., Tarver, S. G., & Jungiohann, K. (2006). *Teaching struggling and at-risk readers: A direct instruction approach.* Upper Saddle River, NJ: Pearson.

Cooper, J. D., Chard, D. J., & Kiger, N. D. (2006). *The struggling reader: Interventions that work.* New York: Scholastic.

Diamond, L., & Gutlohn, L. (2006). *Vocabulary handbook.* Berkeley, CA: Consortium on Reading Excellence, Inc. (CORE).

Goldenberg, C. (2008). Teaching English language learners: What the research does—and does not—say. *American Educator,* Summer, pp. 8–23, 42–44. Retrieved from http://www.aft.org/newspubs/periodicals.

Hirsch, E. D., Jr. (2003). Reading comprehension requires knowledge—of words and the world. *American Educator,* Spring, pp. 10–22, 44. Retrieved from http://www.aft.org/newspubs/periodicals.

Kamil, M. L., & Hiebert E. H. (2005). The teaching and learning of vocabulary: Perspectives and persistent issues. In E. H. Hiebert & M. Kamil (Eds.), *Teaching and learning vocabulary: Bringing scientific research to practice.* Mahwah, NJ: Erlbaum.

Kindle, K. J. (2008). *Teaching vocabulary in the K–2 classroom.* New York: Scholastic.

National Reading Panel (2002). *Teaching children to read: An evidence-based assessment of the scientific research literature.* Washington, DC: National Academy Press.

National Reading Panel (2001). *Put reading first: The research building blocks for teaching children to read.* Washington, DC: National Academy Press.

Scientists at Work (pages 20–24)

PAGE 1
Word Alert! Answers will vary, but should include making a guess about what might happen in the future.

PAGE 3
Vocabulary Comics: predict, classify, observe, measure, infer, communicate

PAGE 4
Syllable Smarties: (*left*) infer, measure, observe, predict; (*right*) classify

Word Hound: 1. communicate; 2. classify; 3. infer; 4. observe

Make a Connection: measurement

PAGE 5
Crossword:

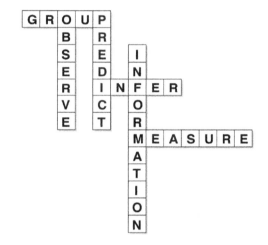

Fun Fact Puzzler: brain

Life Cycles (pages 25–29)

PAGE 1
Word Alert! Answers will vary, but should include changes in the life cycle of a creature.

PAGE 3
Vocabulary Comics: egg, caterpillar, molt, chrysalis, butterfly

PAGE 4
Syllable Smarties: (*left*) egg, molt; (*right*) butterfly, chrysalis

Word Hound: 1. chrysalis; 2. butterfly; 3. metamorphosis; 4. caterpillar

Make a Connection: Answers will vary.

PAGE 5
Crossword:

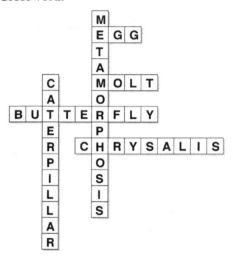

Fun Fact Puzzler: flutter

Food Chains (pages 30–34)

PAGE 1
Word Alert! 1. bakes; 2. glides; 3. consumes

PAGE 3
Vocabulary Comics: producers, consumers, herbivores, carnivores, omnivores

PAGE 4
Syllable Smarties: (*left*) carnivore, consumer, herbivore, omnivore, producer; (*right*) decomposer

Word Hound: 1. omnivore; 2. producer; 3. carnivore; 4. herbivore

Make a Connection: Answers will vary.

PAGE 5
Crossword:

Fun Fact Puzzler: food web

From Seed to Plant (pages 35–39)

PAGE 1
Word Alert! 1. cat; 2. jam

PAGE 3
Vocabulary Comics: seed, embryo, germinate, coat, roots, seedling

PAGE 4
Syllable Smarties: (*left*) coat, roots, seed; (*right*) seedling

Word Hound: 1. seedling; 2. roots; 3. germinate; 4. embryo

Make a Connection: Answers will vary.

PAGE 5
Crossword:

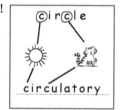

Fun Fact Puzzler: coconut

The Human Body (pages 40–44)

PAGE 1
Word Alert!

PAGE 3
Vocabulary Comics: muscular, digestive, circulatory, immune, respiratory, skeletal

PAGE 4
Syllable Smarties: (*left*) immune; (*right*) digestive, muscular, skeletal

Word Hound: 1. circulatory; 2. immune; 3. muscular; 4. digestive

Make a Connection: skeleton

PAGE 5
Crossword:

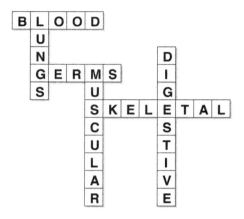

Fun Fact Puzzler: skin

The Five Senses (pages 45–49)

PAGE 1
Word Alert! Answers will vary.

PAGE 3
Vocabulary Comics: smell, taste, hearing, sight, touch, senses

PAGE 4
Syllable Smarties: (*left*) sight, smell, taste, touch; (*right*) hearing, senses

Word Hound: 1. smell; 2. hearing; 3. touch; 4. sight

Make a Connection: Answers will vary.

PAGE 5
Crossword:

Fun Fact Puzzler: earthworm

Extreme Weather! (pages 50–54)

PAGE 1
Word Alert! drizzle, puddle, funnel

PAGE 3
Vocabulary Comics: drought, monsoon, tornado, hurricane, hail, blizzard

PAGE 4
Syllable Smarties: (*left*) blizzard, monsoon; (*right*) hurricane, tornado

Word Hound: 1. drought; 2. monsoon; 3. tornado; 4. hurricane

Make a Connection: Answers will vary.

PAGE 5
Crossword:

Fun Fact Puzzler: hailstone

Planet Protectors (pages 55–59)

PAGE 1
Word Alert! Answers will vary.

PAGE 3
Vocabulary Comics: environment, conserve, resource, compost, recycle

PAGE 4
Syllable Smarties: (*left*) compost, conserve, resource; (*right*) pollution, recycle

Word Hound: 1. pollution; 2. recycle; 3. environment; 4. resource

Make a Connection: Answers will vary.

PAGE 5
Crossword:

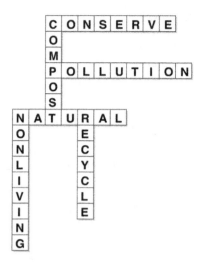

Fun Fact Puzzler: air, water

Objects in Space (pages 60–64)

PAGE 1
Word Alert! meteor

PAGE 3
Vocabulary Comics: galaxy, satellite, asteroid, comet, planet, meteor

PAGE 4
Syllable Smarties: (*left*) comet, planet; (*right*) asteroid, galaxy, meteor, satellite

Word Hound: 1. meteor; 2. satellite; 3. planet; 4. comet

Make a Connection: (*1 million*) 1,000,000; (*1 billion*) 1,000,000,000; (*1 trillion*) 1,000,000,000,000

PAGE 5
Crossword:

Fun Fact Puzzler: black hole

Our Government (pages 65–69)

PAGE 1
Word Alert! rights; answers will vary

PAGE 3
Vocabulary Comics: election, rights, democracy, citizenship, responsibilities, laws

PAGE 4
Syllable Smarties: (*left*) laws, rights; (*right*) election

Word Hound: 1. responsibilities; 2. election; 3. citizenship; 4. rights

Make a Connection: Answers will vary.

PAGE 5
Crossword:

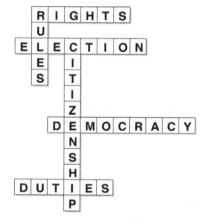

Fun Fact Puzzler: John Adams

Neighborhoods and Communities (pages 70–74)

PAGE 1
Word Alert! 1. suburban; 2. submarine; 3. subzero

PAGE 3
Vocabulary Comics: population, neighborhood, rural, urban, suburban

PAGE 4
Syllable Smarties: (*left*) rural, urban; (*right*) neighborhood, suburban

Word Hound: 1. community; 2. neighborhood; 3. population; 4. suburban

Make a Connection: Answers will vary.

PAGE 5
Crossword:

Fun Fact Puzzler: Census

Customs and Cultures (pages 75–79)

PAGE 1
Word Alert! cus | toms, cul | ture

PAGE 3
Vocabulary Comics: ancestors, diversity, culture, heritage, traditions

PAGE 4
Syllable Smarties: (*left*) customs, culture; (*right*) ancestors, heritage, traditions

Word Hound: 1. traditions; 2. ancestors; 3. diversity; 4. heritage

Make a Connection: Answers will vary.

PAGE 5
Crossword:

Fun Fact Puzzler: rabbit

Maps (pages 80–84)

PAGE 1
Word Alert! 1. part of a fish (or similar answer); 2. used for weighing things (or similar answer)

PAGE 3
Vocabulary Comics: border, legend, scale, compass, longitude

PAGE 4
Syllable Smarties: (*left*) scale (students may also include "rose"; (*right*) border, legend (students may also include "compass")

Word Hound: 1. scale; 2. latitude; 3. legend; 4. longitude

Make a Connection: Answers will vary.

PAGE 5
Crossword:

Fun Fact Puzzler: echolocation

Landforms   (pages 85–89)

PAGE 1
Word Alert! 1. plain; 2. plain, plane

PAGE 3
Vocabulary Comics: plain, mountain, valley, canyon, peninsula, island

PAGE 4
Syllable Smarties: (*left*) plain; (*right*) canyon, island, mountain, valley

Word Hound: 1. plain; 2. island; 3. peninsula; 4. valley

Make a Connection: Answers will vary.

PAGE 5
Crossword:

Fun Fact Puzzler: submarine

Water All Around (pages 90–94)

PAGE 1
Word Alert! 1. pond; 2. sea; 3. stream

PAGE 3
Vocabulary Comics: ocean, gulf, lagoon, river, brook, lake

PAGE 4
Syllable Smarties: (*left*) brook, gulf, lake; (*right*) lagoon, ocean, river

Word Hound: 1. lake; 2. lagoon; 3. river; 4. ocean

Make a Connection: Answers will vary.

PAGE 5
Crossword:

Fun Fact Puzzler: Missouri

To Market, To Market (pages 95–99)

PAGE 1
Word Alert! consumers, goods, producers, services

PAGE 3
Vocabulary Comics: demand, consumers, goods, supply, services, producer

PAGE 4
Syllable Smarties: (*left*) demand, supply; (*right*) consumers, producers, services

Word Hound: 1. goods; 2. supply; 3. demand; 4. services

Make a Connection: Answers will vary.

PAGE 5
Crossword:

Fun Fact Puzzler: touch

American Symbols (pages 100–104)

PAGE 1
Word Alert! Answers will vary.

PAGE 3
Vocabulary Comics: Liberty, Bell, Plymouth, Independence, Constitution, American

PAGE 4
Syllable Smarties: (*left*) liberty; (*right*) American, constitution, declaration

Word Hound: 1. Plymouth; 2. constitution; 3. American; 4. statue

Make a Connection: Answers will vary.

PAGE 5
Crossword:

Fun Fact Puzzler: obelisk

Names for Numbers (pages 105–109)

PAGE 1
Word Alert! 1. odd; 2. even

PAGE 3
Vocabulary Comics: tally, odd, even, digit, Roman, ordinal

PAGE 4
Syllable Smarties: (*left*) odd; (*right*) digit, even, Roman, tally

Word Hound: 1. ordinal; 2. tally; 3. Roman; 4. digit

Make a Connection: Answers will vary.

PAGE 5
Crossword:

Fun Fact Puzzler: googol

Add and Subtract (pages 110–114)

PAGE 1
Word Alert! group; re, ing; do, ing

PAGE 3
Vocabulary Comics: addend, sum, fact, difference, inverse, regrouping

PAGE 4
Syllable Smarties: (*left*) addend, inverse; (*right*) difference, regrouping

Word Hound: 1. difference; 2. regrouping; 3. sum; 4. addend

Make a Connection: Answers will vary.

PAGE 5
Crossword:

Fun Fact Puzzler: abacus

Measuring Time (pages 115–119)

PAGE 1
Word Alert! calendars, decades, months, weeks, years

PAGE 3
Vocabulary Comics: calendar, year, week, month, decade, century

PAGE 4
Syllable Smarties: (*left*) month, week, year; (*right*) calendar, century

Word Hound: 1. year; 2. century; 3. week; 4. decade

Make a Connection: Answers will vary.

PAGE 5
Crossword:

Fun Fact Puzzler: millennium

Multiply and Divide (pages 120–124)

PAGE 1
Word Alert! 1. quotient; 2. quick, quiet, square, equal

PAGE 3
Vocabulary Comics: factor, product, multiple, divisor, quotient, remainder

PAGE 4
Syllable Smarties: (*left*) factor, product, quotient; (*right*) divisor, multiple, remainder

Word Hound: 1. quotient; 2. remainder; 3. divisor; 4. factor

Make a Connection: 15; 15; answers may vary but should reflect understanding that multiplying is quicker than adding

PAGE 5
Crossword:

Fun Fact Puzzler: many times

Fractions (pages 125–129)

PAGE 1
Word Alert! Students should circle the letters in *numerator* and *simplify* (such as *num* and *simp*) that remind them of a word they know, then complete the chart by filling in the words *number* and *simple*.

PAGE 3
Vocabulary Comics: numerator, denominator, fraction bar, mixed, equivalent

PAGE 4
Syllable Smarties: (*left*) fraction; (*right*) denominator

Word Hound: 1. simplify; 2. equivalent; 3. denominator; 4. numerator

Make a Connection: Answers will vary.

PAGE 5
Crossword:

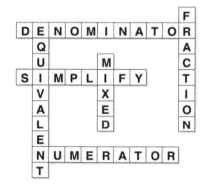

Fun Fact Puzzler: fifteen

Geometry (pages 130–134)

PAGE 1
Word Alert! 1. cheese; 2. rose; 3. stars; 4. pies

PAGE 3
Vocabulary Comics: cylinder, sphere, cube, pyramid, prism, cone

PAGE 4
Syllable Smarties: (*left*) cone, cube, sphere; (*right*) cylinder, pyramid

Word Hound: 1. cone; 2. sphere; 3. cube; 4. pyramid

Make a Connection: Answers will vary.

PAGE 5
Crossword:

Fun Fact Puzzler: toroid

Measurement (pages 135–139)

PAGE 1
Word Alert! weight; answers will vary

PAGE 3
Vocabulary Comics: area, time, length, temperature, weight, volume

PAGE 4
Syllable Smarties: (*left*) length, time, weight; (*right*) area

Word Hound: 1. time; 2. area; 3. weight; 4. length

Make a Connection: Answers will vary.

PAGE 5
Crossword:

Fun Fact Puzzler: leap year

Data Analysis (pages 140–144)

PAGE 1
Word Alert! 1. graph; 2. phone; 3. photo; 4. elephant

PAGE 3
Vocabulary Comics: survey, data, graph, scale, range

PAGE 4
Syllable Smarties: (*left*) graph, range, scale; (*right*) axis, data, survey

Word Hound: 1. scale; 2. graph; 3. range; 4. data

Make a Connection: Answers will vary.

PAGE 5
Crossword:

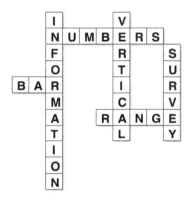

Fun Fact Puzzler: surveyor

Vocabulary Comics

Name: _____ Date: _____

_____
(title)

Instant Content Area Vocabulary Packets © 2011 by Joan Novelli & Holly Grundon, Scholastic Teaching Resources

Make Your Own Comic Strip!

Cut out the speech bubbles you want to use. Write in the shapes, then glue them to your comic strip.

Instant Content Area Vocabulary Packets © 2011 by Joan Novelli & Holly Grundon, Scholastic Teaching Resources **19**

Name: _____ Date: _____

What do you know about the way scientists work? Scientists ask questions and find answers. They use important skills to do this. Look at each word below. Put a ✔ in the box that shows how much you know about that word.

Words to Know

Words	I Know That Word!	It Sounds Familiar...	It's New to Me.
classify			
communicate			
infer			
measure			
observe			
predict			

Word Alert!

You can figure out what some words mean by looking at the word parts. **Predict** has two parts.

Word Part → Meaning	
pre → before	
dict → to say	

Use what you know about **pre** and **dict** to tell what **predict** means. _____

_____

_____

Name: _____   Date: _____

My Mini-Dictionary

Read each word and its meaning. Write a hint or draw a picture to help you learn the word.

classify (KLAS•uh•fye) to sort and group objects by something they have in common

communicate (KUH•myoo•nuh•kate) to share information, for example, by speaking, writing, or drawing

infer (in•FUR) to form an opinion or reach a conclusion using what you know about something

measure (MEZH•ur) to find out the size, length, or amount of something

observe (ub•ZERV) to use your five senses to notice details

predict (pri•DIKT) to use what you know to make a good guess about what might happen in the future

Name: _____   Date: _____

Vocabulary Comics

The Great Paper Airplane Experiment

Complete the sentences in the comic strip. Use the Word Bank for help. Then read the comics!

Word Bank

classify	measure
communicate	observe
infer	predict

Panel 1:
Our paper airplane experiment is going to be topflight. Get it?

Ha, ha. I _____ this Jumbo Jet will win.

Panel 2:
Let's _____ our planes into groups. How about Gliders, Circlers, and Divers?

Panel 3:
I'll carefully _____ what happens when you fly each plane.

Panel 4:
Then I'll _____ the distance each plane goes.

Panel 5:
The Jumbo Jet took a nose dive!

I can _____ the reason for that. Just look at the shape of the wings!

Panel 6:
We'll have to _____ that little problem in our report.

Next time, let's adjust the angle of the wings.

Instant Content Area Vocabulary Packets © 2011 by Joan Novelli & Holly Grundon, Scholastic Teaching Resources

Name: _____ Date: _____

Word Bank

- classify
- communicate
- infer
- measure
- observe
- predict

Syllable Smarties

Read each word in the Word Bank. Count the syllables. Write the words that have 2 syllables and 3 syllables.

Word Hound

Read each clue. Track down the answer! Use the Word Bank.

1. This word has every vowel—**a**, **e**, **i**, **o**, and **u**: _____

2. You can find **class** and **if** in this word: _____

3. This word begins with the opposite of **out**: _____

4. This word begins and ends with a vowel: _____

Make a Connection

Think about the meaning of the word **measure**.
Then complete the sentence by filling in the missing letters.

If you want to find out how tall you are, you can

take a measure ____ ____ ____ ____ .

Name: _____ Date: _____

CROSSWORD

Read each clue. Write the answer in the puzzle. Fill in each box.

Across

1. when you classify things, you sort or _____ them

5. to _____ means to come up with a conclusion

6. you can do this with a ruler

Down

2. your five senses help you do this

3. another word for *guess*

4. communicate means to share _____

Fun Fact Puzzler

Crack the code to learn a fun fact.
First find each shape in the crossword puzzle.
Then write that letter on the line above the shape.

What is an important tool for scientists?

Their ___ ___ ___ ___ ___ !
● ■ ▲ ◆ ★

Name: _____ Date: _____

 What do you know about a butterfly's life cycle? A butterfly lays an egg. A caterpillar hatches from the egg. It goes through changes as it grows. Finally, it becomes a butterfly! Look at each word below. Put a ✔ in the box that shows how much you know about that word.

Words to Know

Words	I Know That Word!	It Sounds Familiar...	It's New to Me.
butterfly			
caterpillar			
chrysalis			
egg			
metamorphosis			
molt			

Word Alert!

You can figure out some tough words—like **metamorphosis**—by looking at the word parts.

Word Part →	Meaning
meta →	change
morph →	form

Use what you know about **meta** and **morph** to tell what butterfly **metamorphosis** is. _____

_____

_____

Name: _____   Date: _____

My Mini-Dictionary

Read each word and its meaning. Write a hint or draw a picture to help you learn the word.

butterfly (BUH•tur•flye) an insect with wings that forms from a caterpillar

caterpillar (KAT•er•pil•er) the wormlike stage of a butterfly; also called the *larva*

chrysalis (KRIS•uh•lis) the stage in which a caterpillar forms a hard outer shell; also called the *pupa*

egg (eg) the first stage of a butterfly's life cycle

metamorphosis (met•uh•MOR•fuh•siss) the changes in form from one stage to the next in a creature's life cycle

molt (molt) to shed old skin to make way for new growth

Name: _____ Date: _____

A Butterfly's Life

Complete the sentences in the comic strip. Use the Word Bank for help. Then read the comics!

Word Bank

butterfly	egg
caterpillar	molt
chrysalis	

I am tiny and round. I am a butterfly _____.

Surprise! I hatched and came out as a _____.

When I'm an adult, I won't look a bit like this!

I eat and eat and grow and grow! When I get too big for my skin, I _____.

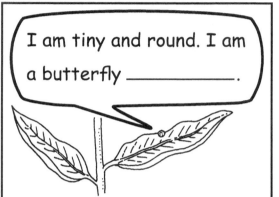

That's better. My new skin is a perfect fit!

I'm a _____ now. My hard shell protects me while big changes happen inside!

I'm finally a _____!
I let my wings dry, and now I can fly!

Name: _____ Date: _____

Word Bank

- butterfly
- caterpillar
- chrysalis
- egg
- metamorphosis
- molt

Syllable Smarties

Read each word in the Word Bank. Count the syllables. Write the words that have 1 syllable and 3 syllables.

Word Hound

Read each clue. Track down the answer! Use the Word Bank.

1. This word begins with five consonants: _____

2. This insect's name is a compound word: _____

3. This word has every vowel but **u**: _____

4. The words **ate** and **ill** are in this word: _____

Make a Connection

Sometimes people say "I have butterflies in my stomach." What do you think that means? (Hint: They don't really have butterflies in their stomachs!)

> I had **butterflies in my stomach** before our school play.

_____

_____

Name: _____   Date: _____

CROSSWORD

Read each clue. Write the answer in the puzzle. Fill in each box.

Across

2. a caterpillar hatches from an _____

4. to shed a layer of skin

5. egg, caterpillar, chrysalis, _____

6. also called the *pupa*

Down

1. the changes in a butterfly's form from egg to adult

3. also called the *larva*

Fun Fact Puzzler

Crack the code to learn a fun fact.
First find each shape in the crossword puzzle.
Then write that letter on the line above the shape.

What's one name for a group of butterflies?

A ___ ___ ___ ___ ___ ___ ___
   ●   ■   ▲   ◆   ◆   ★   ☾

Name: _____ Date: _____

What do you know about food chains? A food chain shows how a group of living things are connected by what they eat. Rabbits eat grass, and snakes eat rabbits. They're both part of the same food chain! Put a ✔ in the box that shows how much you know about that word.

Words to Know

Words	I Know That Word!	It Sounds Familiar...	It's New to Me.
carnivore			
consumer			
decomposer			
herbivore			
omnivore			
producer			

Word Alert! Suffixes are endings that you add to words. Knowing a suffix can help you learn new words.

Suffix →	Meaning
-er →	a person who (or thing that) does something (a skater skates; a computer computes)

Look at some words with the suffix **-er**. Write the missing words.

1. **baker:** someone who _____

2. **glider:** something that _____

3. **consumer:** someone or something that _____

Name: _____ Date: _____

My Mini-Dictionary

Read each word and its meaning. Write a hint or draw a picture to help you learn the word.

carnivore (KAR•nuh•vor) an animal that eats meat

consumer (kun•SOO•mur) a living thing, usually an animal, that eats other living things

decomposer (dee•kum•POH•zur) a living thing, like an earthworm, that breaks down dead materials for food

herbivore (HER•bih•vor) an animal that eats plants

omnivore (OM•nuh•vor) an animal that eats both plants and meat

producer (pruh•DOO•sur) a living thing that makes its own food; plants use sunlight to make their own food

Name: _____ Date: _____

 **Vocabulary Comics**

Dinosaur Diets

Complete the sentences in the comic strip. Use the Word Bank for help. Then read the comics!

Word Bank

carnivores	omnivores
consumers	producers
herbivores	

I am Professor Mosquito, the dinosaur and food chain expert.

Let's begin with plants. Plants are _____. They use sunlight to make their own food.

Unlike plants, dinosaurs were _____. They ate other living things.

Triceratops and many other dinosaurs were plant-eaters. These _____ ate lots of ferns and leaves!

Some dinosaurs, like T-rex, were _____. These meat-eaters had sharp teeth!

Other dinosaurs may have been _____. Many humans eat both plants and animals, too!

Instant Content Area Vocabulary Packets © 2011 by Joan Novelli & Holly Grundon, Scholastic Teaching Resources

Name: _____   Date: _____

Word Bank

- carnivore
- consumer
- decomposer
- herbivore
- omnivore
- producer

Syllable Smarties

Read each word in the Word Bank. Count the syllables. Write the words that have 3 syllables and 4 syllables.

3

4

Word Hound

Read each clue. Track down the answer! Use the Word Bank.

1. This word begins and ends with a vowel: _____

2. Words with the suffix -**er**: **consumer**, **decomposer**, _____

3. This word begins with the little word **car**: _____

4. Fill in the missing letters: ___ **er** ___ **i** ___ **or** ___

Make a Connection

Think about what a **consumer** does.
List things you like to consume.

_____   _____

_____   _____

Name: _____ Date: _____

CROSSWORD

Read each clue. Write the answer in the puzzle. Fill in each box.

Across

3. another name for a plant-eater

5. a _____ eats other living things

6. a carnivore is a _____-eater

Down

1. an animal that eats plants and meat

2. producers make their own _____

4. this decomposer lives in the soil

Fun Fact Puzzler

Crack the code to learn a fun fact.
First find each shape in the crossword puzzle.
Then write that letter on the line above the shape.

Hint: Animals in one food chain eat living things from another.

What is a group of food chains called?

A ___ ___ ___ ___ ___ ___ ___ ___
  ● ■ ■ ◆ ☾ ★ ▲

Name: _____ Date: _____

What do you know about seeds and plants?

Many plants begin as a seed. Look at each word below. Put a ✔ in the box that shows how much you know about that word.

Words to Know

Words	I Know That Word!	It Sounds Familiar...	It's New to Me.
coat			
embryo			
germinate			
roots			
seed			
seedling			

Word Alert!	Some letters have more than one sound. Knowing this can help you figure out new words.

C can sound like...	G can sound like...
the c in cat	the g in goat
or	or
the s in sun	the j in jar

Read each word. Fill in the ◯ for the word with the same beginning sound.

1. coat   ◯ sun   ◯ cat

2. germinate   ◯ jam   ◯ goat

Name: _____   Date: _____

My Mini-Dictionary

Read each word and its meaning. Write a hint or draw a picture to help you learn the word.

coat (kote) the hard, outer covering that protects a seed

embryo (EM•bree•oh) the baby plant inside a seed

germinate (JUR•muh•nate) the stage when a plant begins to grow from a seed

roots (rootz) the part of a plant that grows into the ground and holds it in place

seed (seed) the beginning of a plant; this has a tiny plant inside waiting to grow

seedling (SEED•ling) a young plant

Name: _____   Date: _____

Vocabulary Comics

Inside a Seed

Complete the sentences in the comic strip. Use the Word Bank for help. Then read the comics!

Word Bank	
coat	roots
embryo	seed
germinate	seedling

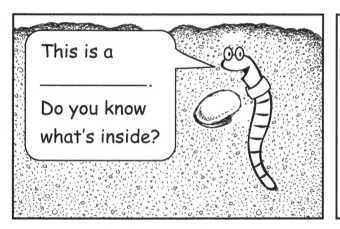

This is a
_____.
Do you know
what's inside?

A tiny plant, called an
_____,
is inside. It's waiting
to grow.

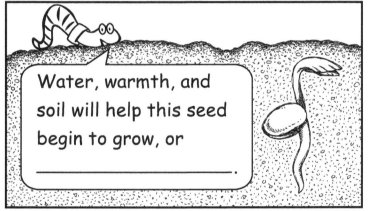

Water, warmth, and
soil will help this seed
begin to grow, or
_____.

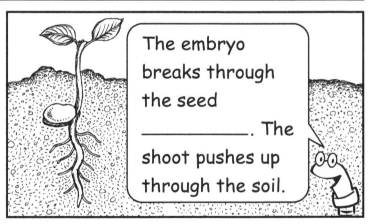

The embryo
breaks through
the seed
_____. The
shoot pushes up
through the soil.

The _____
grow deep in the
ground. Leaves
grow on the stem.

The young plant
is called a
_____.
Can you guess what
it will become?

Name: _____   Date: _____

Word Bank

- coat
- embryo
- germinate
- roots
- seed
- seedling

 **Syllable Smarties** Read each word in the Word Bank. Count the syllables. Write the words that have 1 syllable and 2 syllables.

Word Hound

Read each clue. Track down the answer! Use the Word Bank.

1. The little word **seed** is part of this word: _____

2. Your teeth have these, too: _____

3. Fill in the missing letters: g ___ ___ m ___ ___ a ___ ___

4. This word begins and ends with a vowel: _____

Make a Connection

Think about the **coat** of a seed.
How is that like a coat you wear when it's cold?

_____

_____

Name: _____   Date: _____

CROSSWORD

Read each clue. Write the answer in the puzzle. Fill in each box.

Across

2. a seedling is a _____ plant

4. a plant's roots grow in the _____

5. a baby _____ grows inside a seed

6. what the baby plant inside a seed is called

Down

1. a seed _____ protects the baby plant

3. when a plant begins to grow from a seed: _____

Fun Fact Puzzler

Crack the code to learn a fun fact.
First find each shape in the crossword puzzle.
Then write that letter on the line above the shape.

What is the largest seed in the world?

The double ___ ___ ___ ___ ___ ___ ___
▲   ●   ▲   ●   ■   ◆   ★

Name: _____ Date: _____

What do you know about the human body? The human body has lots of parts. A group of parts is called a **system**. The systems work together to keep the body running. Look at each word below. Put a ✔ in the box that shows how much you know about that word.

Words to Know

Words	I Know That Word!	It Sounds Familiar...	It's New to Me.
circulatory system			
digestive system			
immune system			
muscular system			
respiratory system			
skeletal system			

Word Alert! Some letters have more than one sound. Knowing this can help you read new words.

1. Say the word in the box, then name each picture. Draw a line from each **c** to the picture that has the same sound.

2. Look at Words to Know. Write the word that has **c** two times. Draw a line from each **c** to the matching picture.

ⓒi rⓒl e

Name: _____ Date: _____

My Mini-Dictionary

Read each word and its meaning. Write a hint or draw a picture to help you learn the word.

circulatory (SUR•kyoo•luh•TOR•ee) **system** moves blood through your body

digestive (dye•JES•tiv) **system** breaks down food for your body to use

immune (ih•MYOON) **system** helps your body fight germs and disease

muscular (MUS•kyoo•ler) **system** the network of muscles that control movements of your body

respiratory (RES•pur•uh•TOR•ee) **system** helps you get oxygen from the air you breathe

skeletal (SKEL•eh•tuhl) **system** the bones, ligaments, and tendons that give your body shape and help you move

Name: _____   Date: _____

Vocabulary Comics

It's a Fact!

Complete the sentences in the comic strip. Use the Word Bank for help. Then read the comics!

Word Bank

circulatory	muscular
digestive	respiratory
immune	skeletal

More than 30 muscles in my _____ system help me make a face like this!

My _____ system will take this pizza on a long trip. My small intestine is about 20 feet long!

My _____ system works hard. It pumps blood to every part of my body in less than 60 seconds!

Jokes might help me stay healthy. Scientists think that laughter helps my

_____

system do its job.

Tiny sacs in my lungs fill up with air when I breathe. My

_____

system has 600 million of these!

Wow! Some parts of your _____ system are like mine! My neck has seven bones. Yours does, too!

Instant Content Area Vocabulary Packets © 2011 by Joan Novelli & Holly Grundon, Scholastic Teaching Resources

Name: _____   Date: _____

Word Bank

- circulatory
- digestive
- immune
- muscular
- respiratory
- skeletal

Syllable Smarties

Read each word in the Word Bank. Count the syllables. Write the words that have 2 syllables and 3 syllables.

Word Hound

Read each clue. Track down the answer! Use the Word Bank.

1. These two words end in -**ory**: **respiratory** and _____

2. This word has a double **m**: _____

3. This word has the little word **us** in it: _____

4. This word has two of each vowel—**i** and **e**: _____

Make a Connection

The **skeletal system** is made up of bones, ligaments, and tendons. What is the name for the picture? Fill in the missing letters.

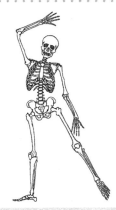

skele ___ ___ ___

Name: _____ Date: _____

CROSSWORD

Read each clue. Write the answer in the puzzle. Fill in each box.

Across

1. your circulatory system pumps this through your body

4. your immune system fights these

6. your _____ system gives your body its shape

Down

2. your _____ fill up with air when you breathe

3. your _____ system breaks down food

5. your _____ system lets you smile or frown

Fun Fact Puzzler

Crack the code to learn a fun fact.
First find each shape in the crossword puzzle.
Then write that letter on the line above the shape.

Sunscreen helps protect this organ.

What is your body's largest organ?

Your ___ ___ ___ ___ !
    ▲   ★   ◆   ●

Name: _____ Date: _____

What do you know about the five senses? You have five sense organs that send information to your brain about the way things sound, look, smell, taste, and feel. Look at each word below. Put a ✔ in the box that shows how much you know about that word.

Words to Know

Words	I Know That Word!	It Sounds Familiar...	It's New to Me.
hearing			
senses			
sight			
smell			
taste			
touch			

Word Alert!

Some words have spelling patterns that are the same. Learning spelling patterns can help you read and write new words.

Look at the word **sight**. In the **-ight** word family, the letters **gh** are silent. Think of more words that have silent **gh**. Write them on the word web.

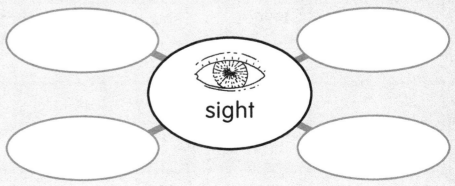

Name: _____ Date: _____

My Mini-Dictionary

Read each word and its meaning. Write a hint or draw a picture to help you learn the word.

hearing (HEER•ing) the ear is the organ that takes in the sounds you hear

senses (SEN•sez) the five ways you can learn about things around you: sight, hearing, taste, smell, and touch

sight (site) the eye is the organ that you use to see things around you; also called *vision*

smell (smel) the nose is the organ that detects odors, or smells

taste (tayst) taste buds in the mouth let you know if something is salty, sweet, bitter, or sour

touch (tuch) the skin is the organ that helps you know about things you touch—for example, the hot, cold, fuzzy, or prickly feel of something

Name: _____   Date: _____

Vocabulary Comics

Midnight Snack
Complete the sentences in the comic strip. Use the Word Bank for help. Then read the comics!

Word Bank

hearing	smell
senses	taste
sight	touch

I'm hungry for a midnight snack. And my sense of _____ tells me there is cheese nearby!

And my sense of _____ tells me it's going to be delicious!

Shhh. That's a cat! Don't make a sound! Cats have a strong sense of _____.

Meow!

Come back! You don't want the cat to see you. Cats have a strong sense of _____, even in the dark.

We're so close, I can almost grab it! My sense of _____ will tell me how smooth and soft it is.

All About Cats

Now, Little Mouse, learning about a cat's five _____ will help you stay safe.

Name: _____ Date: _____

Word Bank

- hearing
- senses
- sight
- smell
- taste
- touch

Syllable Smarties

Read each word in the Word Bank. Count the syllables. Write the words that have 1 syllable and 2 syllables.

Word Hound

Read each clue. Track down the answer! Use the Word Bank.

1. This word ends with a double **l**: _____

2. This word has the little word **ear** in it: _____

3. Take away this word's first letter to spell **ouch**: _____

4. This word rhymes with **night**: _____

Make a Connection

Choose one of the senses: **hearing**, **sight**, **smell**, **taste**, **touch**. Write the word at the center of the word web. Fill in four words that go with that sense.

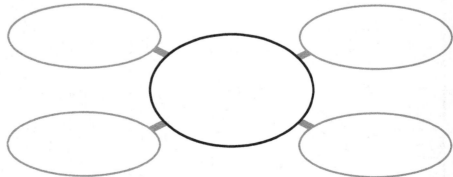

Instant Content Area Vocabulary Packets © 2011 by Joan Novelli & Holly Grundon, Scholastic Teaching Resources

Name: _____   Date: _____

CROSSWORD

Read each clue. Write the answer in the puzzle. Fill in each box.

Across

3. this sense tells you if something is salty or sweet

4. these are your sense _____: eyes, ears, nose, mouth, and skin

Down

1. another word for *sight*

2. your ears are used for this sense

3. this sense lets you feel a puppy's soft fur

5. your sense of _____ can tell you a pie is baking—even if you can't see it

Fun Fact Puzzler

Crack the code to learn a fun fact.
First find each shape in the crossword puzzle.
Then write that letter on the line above the shape.

What animal can taste with its entire body?

An e ___ ___ ___ ___ w ___ ___ ___
       ●   ■   ▲   ◆   ★   ■   ⬡

Name: _____ Date: _____

What do you know about extreme weather? Too much wind, rain, and snow can cause big storms. Too little rainfall can cause big problems, too. Look at each word below. Put a ✔ in the box that shows how much you know about that word.

Words to Know

Words	I Know That Word!	It Sounds Familiar...	It's New to Me.
blizzard			
drought			
hail			
hurricane			
monsoon			
tornado			

Word Alert! Some words have double consonants in the middle. Noticing this can help you read and spell these words.

Double Consonants
blizzard
bliz + zard

Look at the words. Fill in the missing letters.

dri ____ ____ le

pu ____ ____ le

fu ____ ____ el

Name: _____   Date: _____

My Mini-Dictionary

Read each word and its meaning. Write a hint or draw a picture to help you learn the word.

blizzard (BLIZ•urd) a winter storm that has strong winds and heavy snowfall

drought (drout) a long period of time without rain; causes dry, cracked earth and damages plants and crops

hail (hale) small lumps of ice that can form and fall during a thunderstorm

hurricane (HUR•ih•kane) a severe tropical storm with strong circular winds; the "eye" or center is calm

monsoon (mon•SOON) a seasonal wind that usually brings heavy rains

tornado (tor•NAY•doh) a violent, whirling wind that follows a narrow path; also called a *twister* or *funnel cloud*

Name: _____ Date: _____

Vocabulary Comics

What's the Weather?

Complete the sentences in the comic strip. Use the Word Bank for help. Then read the comics!

Word Bank	
blizzard	hurricane
drought	monsoon
hail	tornado

It hasn't rained in more than a month!

My pond is dry. We must be having a _____.

Yikes! This strong wind and heavy rain must mean it's _____ season! Let's go inside.

Duck, do you know what a twister is? That's another name for a _____.

A _____ always starts over a tropical area of the ocean. Many of these powerful storms never make it to land!

I knew water could fall from the clouds during thunderstorms. But sometimes chunks of ice called _____ fall, too.

That's a really cold and heavy snowstorm. It must be a _____. Snow day!

Name: _____   Date: _____

Word Bank

- blizzard
- drought
- hail
- hurricane
- monsoon
- tornado

Syllable Smarties

Read each word in the Word Bank. Count the syllables. Write the words that have 2 syllables and 3 syllables.

Word Hound

Read each clue. Track down the answer! Use the Word Bank.

1. This word rhymes with **shout**: _____

2. This word has the little words **on** and **soon** in it: _____

3. This word begins with **to** and ends with **do**: _____

4. The last letter of this word is silent: _____

Make a Connection

Complete the word web with words that describe a **blizzard**.

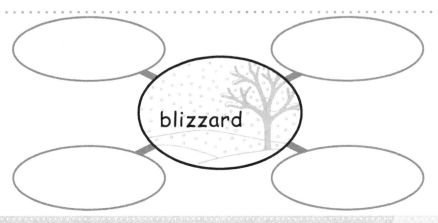

blizzard

Name: _____ Date: _____

CROSSWORD

Read each clue. Write the answer in the puzzle. Fill in each box.

Across

2. also called a *twister*

4. lumps of ice that fall during a thunderstorm

6. a monsoon season is windy and _____

Down

1. a long dry spell that can damage crops

3. a winter storm with strong winds and heavy snow

5. the calm center of a hurricane is the _____

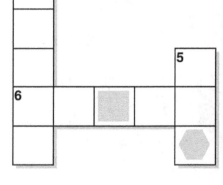

Fun Fact Puzzler

Crack the code to learn a fun fact.
First find each shape in the crossword puzzle.
Then write that letter on the line above the shape.

What is a chunk of hail called?

A h ___ ___ ___ s ___ ___ ___ ___ ___
   ●   ■   ▲   ◆   ☾   ★   ⬡

Name: _____ Date: _____

What do you know about taking care of our planet? There are lots of ways people can help. Look at each word below. Put a ✔ in the box that shows how much you know about that word.

Words to Know

Words	I Know That Word!	It Sounds Familiar...	It's New to Me.
compost			
conserve			
environment			
natural resource			
pollution			
recycle			

Word Alert!

People **recycle** every day. They recycle paper and plastic. They even recycle clothing! Thinking about examples can help you learn new words. Look at the Words below. Write one new example for each word.

Words	Example 1	Example 2
compost	banana peel	
natural resource	trees	
pollution	litter	

Name: _____   Date: _____

My Mini-Dictionary

Read each word and its meaning. Write a hint or draw a picture to help you learn the word.

compost (KOM•pohst) plant parts that rot and break down; improves soil for gardening and farming

conserve (kun•SURV) to use something carefully and wisely; not waste

environment (en•VYE•run•muhnt) the surroundings in which plants and animals live; an environment can have living and nonliving things

natural resource (REE•sors) a material in nature that people use; coal, oil, trees, and water are natural resources

pollution (puh•LOO•shun) the harmful substances and things that make our land, air, or water dirty or unsafe

recycle (ree•SYE•kuhl) to use something again or reuse it in a new way

Name: _____ Date: _____

SuperSquirrel on a Mission

Complete the sentences in the comic strip. Use the Word Bank for help. Then read the comics!

Word Bank

compost	recycle
conserve	resource
environment	

I'm on a mission to protect our _____. My first stop is this school.

This faucet is dripping! I'll turn it off to _____ water.

Coal is a natural _____. We use coal to make electricity. Turning off lights means we use less coal.

ON
OFF

Apple cores over here, everyone! When you use food scraps to make _____, you help keep trash out of landfills.

Compost

Recycle

Put your paper here to _____ it. Thank you! Saving trees helps protect forests for animals like me.

Compost

Recycle

Name: _____ Date: _____

Word Bank

- compost
- conserve
- environment
- pollution
- recycle
- resource

Syllable Smarties

Read each word in the Word Bank. Count the syllables. Write the words that have 2 syllables and 3 syllables.

2

3

Word Hound

Read each clue. Track down the answer! Use the Word Bank.

1. This word has a double l: _____

2. Part of this word is also in **bicycle**: _____

3. Fill in the missing letters: en ___ ___ ron ___ ___ ___ ___

4. The end of this word rhymes with **horse**: _____

Make a Connection

List some important things in your **environment**.

Living things   Nonliving things

_____   _____

_____   _____

Name: _____ Date: _____

Read each clue. Write the answer in the puzzle. Fill in each box.

Across

1. turn water off to save or _____ it

2. litter is a form of _____

3. trees and water are _____ resources

Down

1. made from rotten plant materials

3. an environment has living and _____ things

4. re + cycle = _____

Fun Fact Puzzler

Crack the code to learn a fun fact.
First find each shape in the crossword puzzle.
Then write that letter on the line above the shape.

My leaves help make shade. My roots help keep soil where it belongs.

What two things in nature do trees help make clean?

___ ___ ___   and   w ___ ___ ___ ___

Name: _____ Date: _____

What do you know about objects in space? The sun is the largest object in our solar system. Other objects **orbit**, or travel around, the sun. Look at each word below. Put a ✔ in the box that shows how much you know about that word.

Words to Know

Words	I Know That Word!	It Sounds Familiar...	It's New to Me.
asteroid			
comet			
galaxy			
meteor			
planet			
satellite			

Word Alert! Words that have the same root word may have meanings that are very much alike. Looking for word parts can help you figure out new words.

Look at the two words below. What root word do they share? Write it on the line.

meteorite   meteoroid   _____

Name: _____   Date: _____

My Mini-Dictionary

Read each word and its meaning. Write a hint or draw a picture to help you learn the word.

asteroid (AS•tuh•roid) a rocky object that orbits the Sun; can be from a few feet wide to a hundred miles wide

comet (KOM•it) a chunk of ice, gas, and dust that orbits the Sun; gas and dust often form a tail

galaxy (GAL•uk•see) a huge collection of stars, gas, and dust; our solar system is in the Milky Way galaxy

meteor (MEE•tee•or) a space rock that falls through the sky; sometimes called a *shooting star*

planet (PLAN•it) a large, round body of rock or gas that orbits a star; Earth orbits the Sun, which is a star

satellite (SAT•uh•lite) an object that orbits Earth or another planet; our moon is a satellite

Name: _____   Date: _____

Postcards From Space

Complete the sentences in the comic strip. Use the Word Bank for help. Then read the comics!

Word Bank

asteroid	meteor
comet	planet
galaxy	satellite

I'll take this postcard of our _____, the Milky Way.

Dear Grandma,
The moon looks a lot different up close. Did you know that our moon is a _____ that orbits Earth?

I'm in an _____ belt! Some of these rocky objects are only a few feet wide. But others are wider than the state of New York!

Today I saw a _____ with a long tail. Did you know that asteroids don't have tails?

There's _____ Earth! I'll be home soon.

Look, there's a rock falling through the sky! I'll race that _____. Shooting stars are my favorite!

Name: _____   Date: _____

Word Bank

- asteroid
- comet
- galaxy
- meteor
- planet
- satellite

Syllable Smarties

Read each word in the Word Bank. Count the syllables. Write the words that have 2 syllables and 3 syllables.

Word Hound

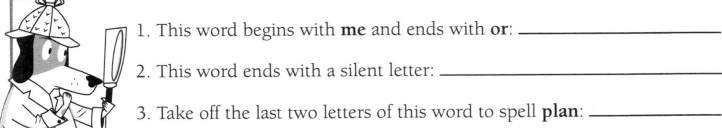

Read each clue. Track down the answer! Use the Word Bank.

1. This word begins with **me** and ends with **or**: _____

2. This word ends with a silent letter: _____

3. Take off the last two letters of this word to spell **plan**: _____

4. Take off the first two letters of this word to spell **met**: _____

Make a Connection

Our **galaxy** has about a trillion stars.
Fill in the blanks with zeroes (0) to write big numbers.

1 million: 1, 000, ___ ___ ___

1 billion: 1, ___ ___ ___ , ___ ___ ___ , ___ ___ ___

1 trillion: 1, ___ ___ ___ , ___ ___ ___ , ___ ___ ___ , ___ ___ ___

Wow! That's a big number!

Name: _____ Date: _____

CROSSWORD

Read each clue. Write the answer in the puzzle. Fill in each box.

Across

2. a meteor is also called a *shooting* _____

4. a large rocky object that orbits the sun

5. this ball of ice and gas has a tail

Down

1. we live on the _____ Earth

2. a moon is a _____ that orbits Earth

3. our solar system is in the _____ Way galaxy

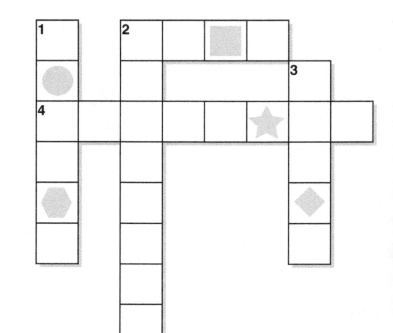

Fun Fact Puzzler

Crack the code to learn a fun fact.
First find each shape in the crossword puzzle.
Then write that letter on the line above the shape.

Objects in space can get pulled into this, but they can't escape it.

A b ___ ___ ___ ___ h ___ ___ ___
  ● ■ ▲ ◆ ★ ● ⬟

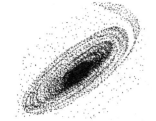

Instant Content Area Vocabulary Packets © 2011 by Joan Novelli & Holly Grundon, Scholastic Teaching Resources

Name: _____ Date: _____

What do you know about our government? A government makes laws about the way a state, country, or other group works. It provides leadership and services. Look at each word below. Put a ✔ in the box that shows how much you know about that word.

Words to Know

Words	I Know That Word!	It Sounds Familiar...	It's New to Me.
citizenship			
democracy			
election			
laws			
responsibilities			
rights			

Word Alert! Homophones are words that sound the same but have different meanings and spellings. The spelling of a homophone helps you know the correct meaning.

Look at Words to Know. Find the missing homophone. Write it on the chart. Think of a new homophone pair. Add the words to the chart.

Homophones		
ate → eight		writes →
one → one		→

Name: _____   Date: _____

My Mini-Dictionary

Read each word and its meaning. Write a hint or draw a picture to help you learn the word.

citizenship (SIT•uh•zuhn•ship) having the rights and responsibilities of people in a group or community

democracy (di•MOK•ruh•see) government by the people; the United States is a democracy

election (ih•LEK•shun) when people vote to choose their leaders; people vote to elect the president of the United States

laws (lawz) the rules made by a government for its people

responsibilities (ri•SPON•suh•BIL•uh•teez) the duties people have to others; people have a duty to respect the rights of others

rights (rites) something that a law says you can have or do; children have the right to go to school and learn

Name: _____ Date: _____

Vocabulary Comics

Election Day!

Complete the sentences in the comic strip. Use the Word Bank for help. Then read the comics!

Word Bank	
citizenship	laws
democracy	responsibilities
election	rights

I'm so excited about our class _____.

I wonder who will be our next president.

I don't know. But I'm glad that voting is one of our _____.

Me, too! Our class is a _____. We get to choose our leaders.

VOTE

VOTE Today!

Voting is a way to show good _____.

VOTE VOTE VOTE Today!

Cleaning up our schoolyard is, too!

So is following the rules and respecting others' property.

Those are called duties or _____. Now let's practice good citizenship and vote!

Hey! Presidents help make _____. I hope our new president makes extra recess a law!

TODAY

Name: _____ Date: _____

Word Bank

citizenship

democracy

election

laws

responsibilities

rights

Syllable Smarties

Read each word in the Word Bank. Count the syllables. Write the words that have 1 syllable and 3 syllables.

Word Hound

Read each clue. Track down the answer! Use the Word Bank.

1. This word has the letter **i** four times: _____

2. This word begins with a vowel: _____

3. This word ends with the small word **ship**: _____

4. This word has a silent **gh**: _____

Make a Connection

Think about the meaning of **citizenship**. List three ways you can show good citizenship.

1. _____

2. _____

3. _____

Name: _____   Date: _____

CROSSWORD

Read each clue. Write the answer in the puzzle. Fill in each box.

Across

1. one of your _____ is to go to school and learn

2. you vote in an _____

4. the type of government in America

5. another word for *responsibilities*

Down

1. another word for *laws*

3. when you help others, you show good _____

Fun Fact Puzzler

Hint: It wasn't George Washington!

Crack the code to learn a fun fact.
First find each shape in the crossword puzzle.
Then write that letter on the line above the shape.

Who was the first president to live in the White House?

President J ___ ___ ___ A ___ ___ ___ ___

● ■ ▲ ◆ ☾ ★ ⬡

Name: _____ Date: _____

What do you know about communities? Your school is part of a community. So is the area where you live. Look at each word below. Put a ✔ in the box that shows how much you know about that word.

Words to Know

Words	I Know That Word!	It Sounds Familiar...	It's New to Me.
community			
neighborhood			
population			
rural			
suburban			
urban			

Word Alert! Prefixes change the meaning of a root word. You can use what you know about prefixes to figure out new words.

Prefix → Meaning	
sub	→ near to, less important than, below, under

Write words with the prefix **sub**. Talk with a friend about the meaning of each word.

1. sub + urban = _____

2. sub + marine = _____

3. sub + zero = _____

Name: _____ Date: _____

My Mini-Dictionary

Read each word and its meaning. Write a hint or draw a picture to help you learn the word.

community (kuh•MYOO•nuh•tee) the group of people who live in a place or area

neighborhood (NAY•bur•hood) the area that surrounds a particular place

population (POP•yuh•LAY•shun) the total number of people (or animals) living in an area

rural (ROO•rel) the country; fewer people live in rural areas than in cities; farms are found in some rural areas

suburban (sub•UR•buhn) an area just outside a city

urban (UR•buhn) a city or large town; people usually live closer together in urban areas than in other areas

Name: _____   Date: _____

Vocabulary Comics

How Many Mice?
Complete the sentences in the comic strip. Use the Word Bank for help. Then read the comics!

Word Bank

neighborhood	suburban
population	urban
rural	

Wow! The _____ of mice might be the highest it's ever been!

To find out, let's count the mice in our community.

Grab your clipboards. Let's go.

Census Tracker

I'll count mice in my _____.

We'll count mice in ours!

We lived in the city before. But we prefer the peace and quiet of our _____ home now.

We lived on a farm before. But we prefer the hustle and bustle of our _____ home now.

We have lived in the city and in the country. But we prefer our _____ home now. It's like having a little of both!

Name: _____ Date: _____

Word Bank

- community
- neighborhood
- population
- rural
- suburban
- urban

 **Syllable Smarties** Read each word in the Word Bank. Count the syllables. Write the words that have 2 syllables and 3 syllables.

Word Hound

Read each clue. Track down the answer! Use the Word Bank.

1. This word has a double **m**: _____

2. This word has a silent **gh**: _____

3. This word has the suffix **-tion**: _____

4. This word begins with the prefix **sub-**: _____

Make a Connection

1. Read the words in the center of the word web. Circle the word that best describes where you live.

2. Write words that tell about this place.

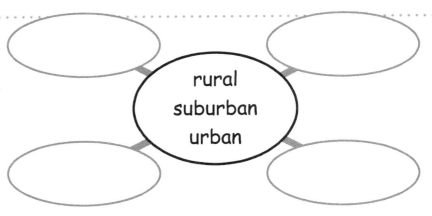

rural
suburban
urban

Name: _____ Date: _____

CROSSWORD

Read each clue. Write the answer in the puzzle. Fill in each box.

Across

2. your _____ is the area around where you live

3. another word for *city*

4. you can find these in many rural areas

6. the group of people who live in an area

Down

1. the total number of people who live in an area

5. a _____ area is just outside a city

Fun Fact Puzzler

Crack the code to learn a fun fact.
First find each shape in the crossword puzzle.
Then write that letter on the line above the shape.

How many people live in your household?

What is used to count the total number of people in our country?

The U.S. ___ ___ ___ ___ ___ ___
●   ■   ▲   ★   ☾   ★

Name: _____ Date: _____

What do you know about customs and cultures? People in your community and around the world have different customs and cultures. Look at each word below. Put a ✔ in the box that shows how much you know about that word.

Words to Know

Words	I Know That Word!	It Sounds Familiar...	It's New to Me.
ancestors			
customs			
culture			
diversity			
heritage			
traditions			

Word Alert!

Breaking words into syllables can be a good way to figure out how to pronounce longer words.

If you see two consonants together in the middle of the word, you can usually divide the word between the consonants. Try it with the words in the chart.

Word	Syllables
ancestors	an | ces | tors
customs	
culture	

Name: _____ Date: _____

My Mini-Dictionary

Read each word and its meaning. Write a hint or draw a picture to help you learn the word.

ancestors (AN•sess•turz) people in your family who lived long before you

customs (KUS•tumz) the way a group of people usually behaves or does things; giving birthday gifts is a custom for many families

culture (KUL•chur) the beliefs, traditions, language, clothing, and activities of a group of people

diversity (di•VUR•suh•tee) being different, or not like others; there is diversity among people and cultures in our world

heritage (HEHR•uh•tij) property, values, and traditions that people pass on to others in their family

traditions (truh•DI•shunz) the customs and beliefs that are handed down from one person (or group of people) to another

Name: _____   Date: _____

Then and Now

Complete the sentences in the comic strip. Use the Word Bank for help. Then read the comics!

Word Bank

ancestors	heritage
culture	traditions
diversity	

I hope we get an A+ on our Pilgrims report.

This time machine will take us back to Colonial America. We'll meet people who lived long ago.

In 1620, the Pilgrims sailed from England to America on the Mayflower. Some people's _____ were Pilgrims.

Our family is from England. Where are you from?

I live in New York. But I moved there from Japan.

The Pilgrims were all from England. Our communities have much more _____ now.

I like your outfit.

Kids my age dress like the grown-ups do.

The way people dress is part of their _____.

We spend the day working with our families. I help plant the fields and tend the animals.

We spend the day at school.

Learning the value of hard work was part of a Pilgrim child's _____.

This table full of food looks familiar.

We're celebrating the harvest with our friends. It's a feast of thanksgiving.

Celebrating Thanksgiving Day is now one of our country's _____.

Name: _____ Date: _____

Word Bank

- ancestors
- customs
- culture
- diversity
- heritage
- traditions

Syllable Smarties

Read each word in the Word Bank. Count the syllables. Write the words that have 2 syllables and 3 syllables.

Word Hound

Read each clue. Track down the answer! Use the Word Bank.

1. This word has **t** and **i** two times each: _____

2. The **c** in this word sounds like the **c** in **city**: _____

3. This word comes from the word **diverse**: _____

4. This word has the little word **age** in it: _____

Make a Connection

Art and music are part of people's **culture**. Tell about art or music that you like.

_____

_____

Name: _____ Date: _____

CROSSWORD

Read each clue. Write the answer in the puzzle. Fill in each box.

Across

2. diversity is about how people are _____

3. art and music are part of a group's _____

5. ancestors are people who lived _____ you

Down

1. where people in a family are from is part of their _____

3. the habits or behaviors of a group of people

4. the way a family always celebrates a special day is a _____

Fun Fact Puzzler

Crack the code to learn a fun fact.
First find each shape in the crossword puzzle.
Then write that letter on the line above the shape.

My ancestors could hop!

Animals have ancestors, too!
How big were an elephant's ancestors?

No bigger than a ___ ___ ___ ___ ___ ___ !
                ●   ■   ▲   ▲   ★   ◆

Name: _____ Date: _____

What do you know about maps? A map is a drawing of an area of land. People use maps to find the location of things like lakes, roads, and towns. Look at each word below. Put a ✔ in the box that shows how much you know about that word.

Words to Know

Words	I Know That Word!	It Sounds Familiar...	It's New to Me.
border			
compass rose			
latitude			
legend			
longitude			
scale			

Word Alert! Some words have more than one meaning. Knowing a word's different meanings can help you understand how the word is being used.

A **scale** is part of a map. The word *scale* has other meanings, too. Look at each picture. Tell what the word *scale* means.

1.  _____

2.  _____

Name: _____   Date: _____

My Mini-Dictionary

Read each word and its meaning. Write a hint or draw a picture to help you learn the word.

border (BOR•dur) shows where an area begins and ends; a boundary

compass rose (KUHM•puhss roze) the arrows on a map that show North, South, East, and West

latitude (LAT•uh•tood) imaginary lines on a map that run east and west

legend (LEJ•uhnd) explains what the symbols on a map mean; also called a *map key*

longitude (LON•juh•tood) imaginary lines that run north and south

scale (skale) a line of marks used to measure distance on a map; an inch on a map scale might equal one mile in actual distance

Name: _____ Date: _____

 **Vocabulary Comics**

Dog and Bone
Complete the sentences in the comic strip. Use the Word Bank for help. Then read the comics!

Everyone knows dogs bury bones. Then they dig up the yard looking for them! I'll be smart and make a map.

First, I'll mark where my yard begins and ends. This will be the _____ of my map.

I'll use symbols to show my shade tree and doghouse. The map _____ will explain what these are.

My map is a drawing of my yard. This _____ will show the actual distances.
0 10 20 30 40 50
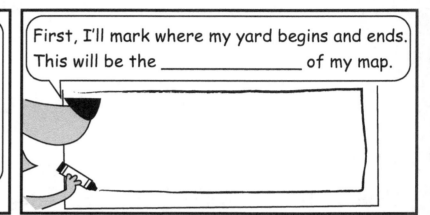

A _____ rose will help me know what direction to go in. It points out North, South, East, and West.

Finally, I'll add lines of latitude and _____ to help me mark the spot. Perfect!

Name: _____   Date: _____

Word Bank

- border
- compass rose
- latitude
- legend
- longitude
- scale

Syllable Smarties

Read each word in the Word Bank. Count the syllables. Write the words that have 1 syllable and 2 syllables.

1

2

Word Hound

Read each clue. Track down the answer! Use the Word Bank.

1. This word rhymes with **whale**: _____

2. This word has every vowel but **o**: _____

3. Three letters at the end of this word spell **end**: _____

4. This word has the little word **long** in it: _____

Make a Connection

The **legend** shows symbols for things that are found on a map. Pretend you are making a map of your classroom. Draw and label symbols for three things in the room.

☐ _____

☐ _____

☐ _____

Name: _____   Date: _____

CROSSWORD

Read each clue. Write the answer in the puzzle. Fill in each box.

Across

2. this part of a map helps you measure distance

5. a border is where an area _____ and ends

6. lines of longitude run _____ and south

Down

1. lines of latitude run east and _____

3. a _____ rose tells directions

4. this explains the symbols on a map

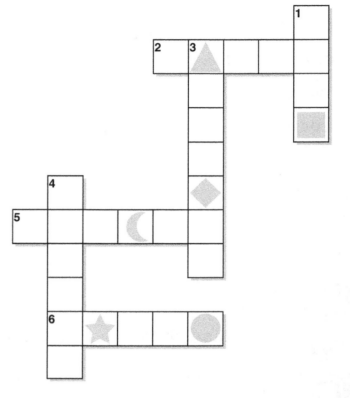

Fun Fact Puzzler

Crack the code to learn a fun fact.
First find each shape in the crossword puzzle.
Then write that letter on the line above the shape.

How do scientists make maps of the ocean floor?

They use e __ __ __ l __ __ __ __ __ __ n.
▲ ● ★ ★ ▲ ◆ ■ ☾ ★

Name: _____ Date: _____

What do you know about landforms? Landforms are the different shapes and types of land found on Earth's surface. Look at each word below. Put a ✔ in the box that shows how much you know about that word.

Words to Know

Words	I Know That Word!	It Sounds Familiar...	It's New to Me.
canyon			
island			
mountain			
peninsula			
plain			
valley			

Word Alert! Some words are homophones. They sound alike but have different spellings and meanings.

1. Look at the word below. Write its homophone from Words to Know.

plane _____

2. Use the homophones **plane** and **plain** to complete the sentence.

The _____ was so large and flat you could land a _____ on it.

Name: _____   Date: _____

My Mini-Dictionary   Read each word and its meaning. Write a hint or draw a picture to help you learn the word.

canyon (KAN•yuhn) a deep, narrow valley with high, steep sides; often carved into the land by a river

island (EYE•luhnd) land that is surrounded on all sides by water

mountain (MOUN•tuhn) land that is much higher than the area around it; usually steeper than a hill

peninsula (puh•NIN•suh•luh) land that sticks out into water like an arm; surrounded by water on three sides

plain (plane) a large, flat area of land; a *plateau* (pla•TOH) is like a plain but higher than the land around it

valley (VAL•ee) low land between hills or mountains

Name: _____   Date: _____

From Here to There

Complete the sentences in the comic strip. Use the Word Bank for help. Then read the comics!

Word Bank

canyon	peninsula
island	plain
mountain	valley

Excuse me, Ant. Can you tell me how to get to Snail's house?

You bet!

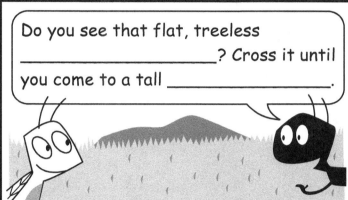

Do you see that flat, treeless _____? Cross it until you come to a tall _____.

Then go through the low land, or _____, between the next two mountains.

You'll come to a deep valley with high, steep sides. Be careful crossing this _____!

At the lake, look for an arm-shaped piece of land that has water on three sides. Go to the end of this _____.

From there, take the boat. Snail's home is on land surrounded on all sides by water. He lives on an _____!

Name: _____ Date: _____

Word Bank

- canyon
- island
- mountain
- peninsula
- plain
- valley

Syllable Smarties Read each word in the Word Bank. Count the syllables. Write the words that have 1 syllable and 2 syllables.

Word Hound

Read each clue. Track down the answer! Use the Word Bank.

1. This word has the long **a** sound: _____

2. The **s** in this word is silent: _____

3. Fill in the missing vowels: p ___ n ___ ns ___ l ___

4. This word has a double letter: _____

Make a Connection

Choose a landform from the Word Bank. Write it at the center of the word web. Fill in words that tell about that landform.

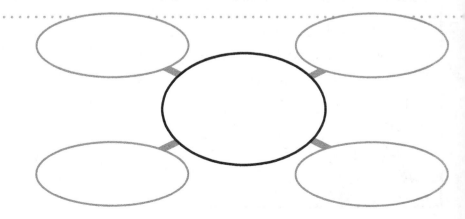

Name: _____   Date: _____

CROSSWORD

Read each clue. Write the answer in the puzzle. Fill in each box.

Across

2. a deep valley with steep sides

5. a mountain is like this but much higher

6. a plateau is _____ than the land around it

Down

1. a valley lies between hills or _____

3. this is surrounded by water on all sides

4. a peninsula has water on _____ sides

Fun Fact Puzzler

Crack the code to learn a fun fact.
First find each shape in the crossword puzzle.
Then write that letter on the line above the shape.

What is the name for a canyon that forms on the ocean floor?

A s __ b __ __ __ __ __ __ canyon
      ●   ▲   ◆   ☾   ★   ■   ⬡

Name: _____ Date: _____

What do you know about bodies of water? There are many names for bodies of water. Look at each word below. Put a ✔ in the box that shows how much you know about that word.

Words to Know

Words	I Know That Word!	It Sounds Familiar...	It's New to Me.
brook			
gulf			
lagoon			
lake			
ocean			
river			

Word Alert!

Some words go together. They name things that are a lot alike. Draw a line to match each body of water to the one that is most like it.

1. lake   stream

2. ocean   pond

3. river   sea

Name: _____   Date: _____

My Mini-Dictionary

Read each word and its meaning. Write a hint or draw a picture to help you learn the word.

brook (brook) a small stream of fresh water; also called a *creek*; sometimes flows into a river

gulf (gulf) a shoreline area of ocean surrounded partly by land; a *bay* is smaller than a gulf

lagoon (luh•GOON) a shallow, salty body of water near a coast; separated from the ocean by reefs or sandbars

lake (lake) a large body of water— usually fresh water—surrounded by land; a *pond* is a small lake

ocean (OH•shun) a large body of salt water; a *sea* can be part of an ocean

river (RIV•ur) a large, flowing body of water; a large *stream*; rivers can flow into lakes or oceans

Name: _____   Date: _____

Vocabulary Comics

Loon's Lake

Complete the sentences in the comic strip. Use the Word Bank for help. Then read the comics!

Word Bank

brook	lagoon
gulf	ocean
lake	river

I live by the _____ in winter. But it is salty and rough. When spring comes, I'll want to build my nest near calm, fresh water.

This _____ is mostly surrounded by land, but it is still part of the salty sea. It will not do for nesting.

This _____ is separated from the sea by a sandbar. But it is too shallow. I need deep water to dive for food.

Look at that log being carried away! This wide _____ flows much too fast for a young loon.

This small stream of fresh water looks safe. But this _____ flows like a river. It will not do for nesting.

This deep, fresh water has land all around it. My chicks will love it here. It's the perfect _____ for nesting.

Name: _____ Date: _____

Word Bank

- brook
- gulf
- lagoon
- lake
- ocean
- river

Syllable Smarties Read each word in the Word Bank. Count the syllables. Write the words that have 1 syllable and 2 syllables.

Word Hound

Read each clue. Track down the answer! Use the Word Bank.

1. This word rhymes with **cake** and **take**: _____

2. Fill in the missing vowels: l __ g __ __ n

3. Unscramble **r e r v i** to spell this word: _____

4. This word has the sound of **sh** in it: _____

Make a Connection

What are some bodies of water you know? Write their names.

A lake: _____

An ocean: _____

A river: _____

Name: _____   Date: _____

CROSSWORD

Read each clue. Write the answer in the puzzle. Fill in each box.

Across

1. another word for *creek*
3. a lake is surrounded by land on all _____
4. a bay is smaller than a _____
5. the Atlantic _____

Down

2. this can flow into a lake or ocean
3. a lagoon is not deep; it is _____

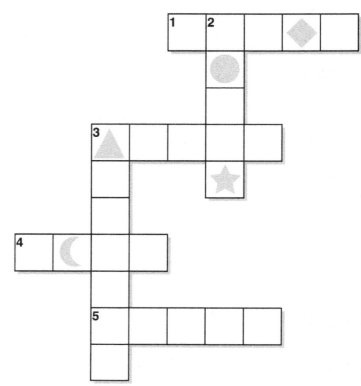

Fun Fact Puzzler

Crack the code to learn a fun fact.
First find each shape in the crossword puzzle.
Then write that letter on the line above the shape.

Hint: It is not the *largest* river!

What is the longest river in the United States?

The M ___ ___ ___ ___ ___ ___ ___ River
      ●   ▲   ▲   ◆   ☾   ★   ●

Name: _____ Date: _____

What do you know about buying and selling? Storekeepers stock different items to sell. Then people buy the things they want or need. Look at each word below. Put a ✔ in the box that shows how much you know about that word.

Words to Know

Words	I Know That Word!	It Sounds Familiar...	It's New to Me.
consumers			
demand			
goods			
producers			
services			
supply			

Word Alert!

To make most nouns plural, you just add **s**: lemon + s = lemons.

Look at Words to Know. Find the plural for each word in the chart. Write it in the box on the right.

Word	Plural
consumer	
good	
producer	
service	

Name: _____ Date: _____

My Mini-Dictionary

Read each word and its meaning. Write a hint or draw a picture to help you learn the word.

consumers (kun•SOO•murz) the people who buy and use goods or services

demand (dee•MAND) how much people want or need a good or service

goods (goodz) items that people buy or sell; goods can be made (like clothes) or grown (like peaches)

producers (pruh•DOO•surz) the people who make goods (like toys) or provide services (like cutting hair)

services (SUR•viss•ez) work that is done for customers; babysitters provide a service to families with children

supply (suh•PLYE) how much of a good or service is available

Name: _____   Date: _____

Vocabulary Comics

Lemonade Stand

Complete the sentences in the comic strip. Use the Word Bank for help. Then read the comics!

Word Bank

consumers	producer
demand	services
goods	supply

So, you want to have a lemonade stand? Cool! There will be a big _____ for that today!

Location, location, location! A busy spot means plenty of _____ to buy your lemonade.

You might like to sell other _____, too. I suggest lemon squares, lemon tarts, and lemon ice pops.

Be sure to make enough of everything. You don't want your _____ to run out too soon.

You want your business to be the best. So, here's a tip: Offer special _____ to your customers.

Sprinkler Service

Bet you're wondering who's going to do all this work. A _____ is someone who makes things to sell. That's you!

To Do:
Squeeze lemons
Bake lemon squares
Bake lemon tarts
Make lemon ice pops
Buy cups
Make sign

Name: _____   Date: _____

Word Bank

- consumers
- demand
- goods
- producers
- services
- supply

Syllable Smarties

Read each word in the Word Bank. Count the syllables. Write the words that have 2 syllables and 3 syllables.

Word Hound

Read each clue. Track down the answer! Use the Word Bank.

1. This word has a double **o**: _____

2. The end of this word rhymes with **fly**: _____

3. This word begins and ends with **d**: _____

4. You can spell **rice** and **ice** with letters in this word: _____

Make a Connection

Think about what **services** are. Fill in the word web to name four services that help you.

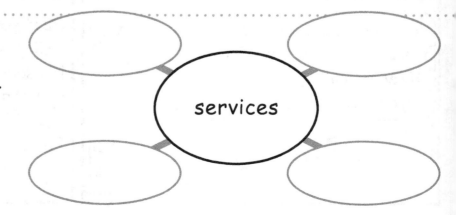

services

Name: _____   Date: _____

CROSSWORD

Read each clue. Write the answer in the puzzle. Fill in each box.

Across

2. demand is how much people _____ or need something

4. _____ are people who buy or use goods or services

5. _____ make goods or provide services

Down

1. the service a barber provides: cutting _____

3. people make and sell baked _____ at a bakery

6. a bike store has a _____ of bikes to sell

Fun Fact Puzzler

Crack the code to learn a fun fact.
First find each shape in the crossword puzzle.
Then write that letter on the line above the shape.

What's the difference between goods and services?

You can't ____ ____ ____ ____ ____ services.
     ●   ■   ★   ▲   ◆

Name: _____ Date: _____

What do you know about symbols of America?
The American flag is one symbol you have probably seen.
Look at each word below. Put a ✔ in the box that shows
how much you know about that word.

Words to Know

Words	I Know That Word!	It Sounds Familiar...	It's New to Me.
American flag			
Declaration of Independence			
Liberty Bell			
Plymouth Rock			
Statue of Liberty			
U.S. Constitution			

Word Alert! A proper noun names a specific person, place, or thing.
Liberty Bell is a proper noun. It begins with capital letters.

Write proper nouns you know.

A friend's name: _____

Your state: _____

Your birthday month: _____

Name: _____   Date: _____

My Mini-Dictionary
Read each word and its meaning. Write a hint or draw a picture to help you learn the word.

American flag the U. S. flag has 50 stars (one for each state) and 13 stripes (one for each original colony)

Declaration of Independence a statement of freedom from Great Britain's rule; written by Thomas Jefferson

Liberty Bell a symbol that celebrates freedom; it is said that this bell was rung when the Declaration of Independence was read in 1776

Plymouth Rock the Pilgrims are said to have landed by this famous rock when the *Mayflower* reached America in 1620

Statue of Liberty a symbol of freedom and democracy (equality); given to the U. S. by the people of France

U.S. Constitution the laws that govern our nation; the first ten amendments are called the *Bill of Rights*

Name: _____   Date: _____

Field Trip!

Complete the sentences in the comic strip. Use the Word Bank for help. Then read the comics!

Word Bank

American	Independence
Bell	Liberty
Constitution	Plymouth

Ready for our field trip to planet Earth? First stop—the United States of America. Let's review.

This symbol of freedom is . . .

. . . the Statue of _____! It was sent over in 350 pieces on a boat from France.

In Philadelphia, we'll see the Liberty _____.

The crack is more than two feet long!

After that, we'll see this famous rock in Massachusetts.

1620

It's _____ Rock! This is known as the landing place of the Pilgrims.

Then, we're off to Washington, DC.

We'll see the Declaration of _____ and the U.S. _____.

"When in the course..."   "We the People..."

Remember when we saw the _____ flag on the moon? Now we'll see it in America!

Name: _____   Date: _____

Word Bank

American

constitution

declaration

liberty

Plymouth

statue

Syllable Smarties

Read each word in the Word Bank. Count the syllables. Write the words that have 3 syllables and 4 syllables.

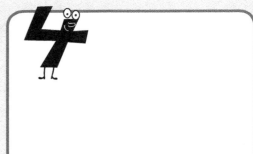

Word Hound

Read each clue. Track down the answer! Use the Word Bank.

1. Fill in the missing letters: Pl ____ mou ____ ____

2. The letter **t** is found 3 times in this word: _____

3. This word has the little word **can** in it: _____

4. Take out the **u** in this word and it spells **state**: _____

Make a Connection

The **Statue of Liberty** is a symbol of freedom. If you could create a statue for America, what would it be? What would it symbolize?

_____

_____

Name: _____ Date: _____

CROSSWORD

Read each clue. Write the answer in the puzzle. Fill in each box.

Across

2. the Statue of _____

6. the Constitution of the _____ States

Down

1. Thomas Jefferson wrote the _____ of Independence

3. the Liberty _____ rings for freedom

4. Plymouth _____ is a famous landmark

5. the American flag has one star for each _____

Fun Fact Puzzler

Crack the code to learn a fun fact.
First find each shape in the crossword puzzle.
Then write that letter on the line above the shape.

**The Washington Monument is another symbol of America.
What is the name for the shape of this landmark?**

An ___ ___ ___ ___ ___ ___ ___
    ■   ●   ▲   ◆   ☾   ★   ⬡

Name: _____ Date: _____

What do you know about numbers? Different words are used to describe numbers. Look at each word below. Put a ✔ in the box that shows how much you know about that word.

Words to Know

Words	I Know That Word!	It Sounds Familiar...	It's New to Me.
digit			
even number			
odd number			
ordinal number			
Roman numeral			
tally marks			

Word Alert! Some words have more than one meaning. A number can be **even** (like 6) or **odd** (like 5). The words *even* and *odd* have other meanings, too. Knowing this can help you choose the correct meaning when you read.

Fill in **even** or **odd** to complete each sentence.

1. It would be _____ to see a moose in a city.

2. I'm going out to play, _____ though it's raining.

Name: _____ Date: _____

My Mini-Dictionary

Read each word and its meaning. Write a hint or draw a picture to help you learn the word.

digit (DIJ•it) the numbers 0, 1, 2, 3, 4, 5, 6, 7, 8, and 9; the number 14 has two digits—1 and 4

even (EE•vuhn) **number** a whole number that can be divided by two: 2, 4, 6, 8, or any number ending in 0, 2, 4, 6, 8

odd (od) **number** a whole number that can't be divided by two: 1, 3, 5, 7, 9, or any number ending in 1, 3, 5, 7, 9

ordinal (ORD•uhn•uhl) **number** a number that names the position or place in an ordered set; *first*, *second*, and *third* are ordinal numbers

Roman (ROH•muhn) **numeral** letters from the Roman alphabet that stand for numbers; I (1), V (5), X (10), L (50), C (100)

tally (TAL•ee) **marks** short lines or marks used to keep count or to keep score; each mark usually counts as one

Name: _____ Date: _____

Vocabulary Comics

Number Collector

Complete the sentences in the comic strip. Use the Word Bank for help. Then read the comics!

Word Bank

digit	ordinal
even	Roman
odd	tally

Some people collect marbles or coins. I collect numbers, numbers, and more numbers! I use _____ marks to keep track of every number in my collection.

I collect _____ numbers, like 3, 7, and 51.

I collect _____ numbers, too, like 4, 6, and 14.

Will Return at 6 — JULY 4

Next Stop 14 miles

Books have numbers on every page. This one goes all the way to 320. That's a triple-_____ number!

Wow!

These capital letters are _____ numerals. Each letter stands for a number.

XXV — Henry the VIII

Naturally, my collection has won many contests. And every prize ribbon has an _____ number on it!

Name: _____   Date: _____

Word Bank

- digit
- even
- odd
- ordinal
- Roman
- tally

Syllable Smarties Read each word in the Word Bank. Count the syllables. Write the words that have 1 syllable and 2 syllables.

Word Hound

Read each clue. Track down the answer! Use the Word Bank.

1. This word contains the little words **or** and **in**: _____

2. The first three letters of this word spell **tall**: _____

3. This word is a proper noun: _____

4. Fill in the missing vowels: d ___ g ___ t

Make a Connection

Write the **Roman numerals** for numbers you know.
Use the key to help you.

My age: _____   My grade: _____

Key	
I = 1	VI = 6
II = 2	VII = 7
III = 3	VIII = 8
IV = 4	IX = 9
V = 5	X = 10

Name: _____   Date: _____

CROSSWORD

Read each clue. Write the answer in the puzzle. Fill in each box.

Across

3. XV is the _____ numeral for 15

4. 5 and 7 are _____ numbers

6. these are _____ marks: ☰☰☰

Down

1. 2 and 4 are _____ numbers

2. *first*, *second*, and *third* are _____ numbers

5. 23 is a two-_____ number

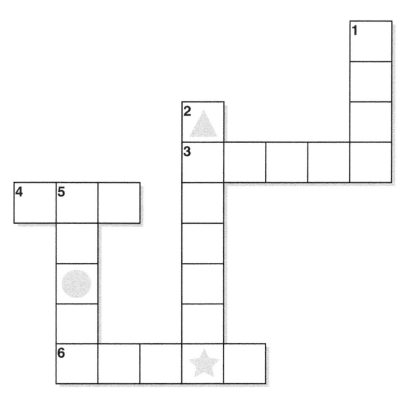

Fun Fact Puzzler

Crack the code to learn a fun fact. First find each shape in the crossword puzzle. Then write that letter on the line above the shape.

What is the name for a very large number that has a 1 followed by 100 zeroes?

A ___ ___ ___ ___ ___ ___
  ● ▲ ▲ ● ▲ ★

Name: _____   Date: _____

What do you know about addition and subtraction? You add to find the total number of two or more sets that are put together. You subtract to find out how many items in a group are left when some are taken away. Look at each word below. Put a ✔ in the box that shows how much you know about that word.

Words to Know

Words	I Know That Word!	It Sounds Familiar...	It's New to Me.
addend			
difference			
fact family			
inverse			
regrouping			
sum			

Word Alert! Some words have a prefix and a suffix. You can break the word into parts to figure out the root word. Fill in the missing word parts.

Words	Prefix	Root	Suffix
regrouping	re		ing
reprinting		print	
redoing	re		

Name: _____ Date: _____

My Mini-Dictionary

Read each word and its meaning. Write a hint or draw a picture to help you learn the word.

addend (AD•end) a number that is added to another number

difference (DIF•ur•ens) the answer in a subtraction problem

fact (fakt) **family** addition and subtraction facts that use the same set of numbers (example: 3 + 5 = 8, 5 + 3 = 8, 8 − 5 = 3, 8 − 3 = 5)

inverse (IN•vurs) opposite; addition and subtraction are inverse operations—they undo each other

regrouping (ree•GROOP•ing) to group a number in another way; 25 is 2 tens and 5 ones, but it can be regrouped as 1 ten and 15 ones

sum (sum) the answer in an addition problem

Name: _____ Date: _____

Vocabulary Comics

Math Mastermind I

Complete the sentences in the comic strip. Use the Word Bank for help. Then read the comics!

Word Bank

addend	inverse
difference	regrouping
fact	sum

Welcome to Math Mastermind! Today, our clues are about addition and subtraction. For 50 points, the first clue . . .

What is an _____?

$$7 + 8 = 15$$

Right! Now for 100 points, . . .

$$10 + 8 = 18$$

What is the _____?

Yes! And for 200 . . .

What is a _____ family?

$$3 + 5 = 8 \quad 8 - 3 = 5$$
$$5 + 3 = 8 \quad 8 - 5 = 3$$

Right again! For 300 . . .

What is the _____?

$$22 - 12 = 10$$

Yes! Now for 400 . . .

What is _____?

Addition and subtraction are **?** operations.

Correct! And our final clue . . .

What is _____?

42 → 4 tens 2 ones
OR
→ 3 tens 12 ones

Good job!

Name: _____ Date: _____

Word Bank

- addend
- difference
- fact
- inverse
- regrouping
- sum

 **Syllable Smarties**

Read each word in the Word Bank. Count the syllables. Write the words that have 2 syllables and 3 syllables.

 **Word Hound**

Read each clue. Track down the answer! Use the Word Bank.

1. This word contains the word **differ**: _____

2. This word has a prefix and a suffix: _____

3. This word rhymes with **hum** and **drum**: _____

4. This word has the letter **d** three times: _____

Make a Connection

When, in real life, do you need to find the **sum** of two or more things? Write about two ideas.

1. _____

2. _____

Name: _____ Date: _____

CROSSWORD

Read each clue. Write the answer in the puzzle. Fill in each box.

Across

3. a number added to another number

5. in 5 + 5 = 10, the _____ is 10

6. this means *opposite*

Down

1. this is a fact _____: 4 + 5 = 9, 5 + 4 = 9, 9 – 5 = 4, and 9 – 4 = 5

2. to group a number in a different way

4. the _____ of 11 – 5 is 6

Fun Fact Puzzler

Crack the code to learn a fun fact.
First find each shape in the crossword puzzle.
Then write that letter on the line above the shape.

People slide counters or beads on this to add and subtract. What is it?

An __ b __ __ __ __
    ●   ●   ▲   ◆   ★

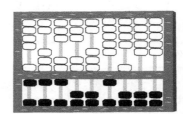

Name: _____ Date: _____

What do you know about measuring time? People measure time in small units like seconds, minutes, and hours. They also use larger units like days, weeks, and months. Put a ✔ in the box that shows how much you know about that word.

Words to Know

Words	I Know That Word!	It Sounds Familiar...	It's New to Me.
calendar			
century			
decade			
month			
week			
year			

Word Alert!

To make most nouns plural, you just add **s**. Add **s** to make each word in the chart plural. Write and read the new words.

Word	+ s	Plural
calendar	+ s	
decade	+ s	
month	+ s	
week	+ s	
year	+ s	

Name: _____   Date: _____

My Mini-Dictionary

Read each word and its meaning. Write a hint or draw a picture to help you learn the word.

calendar (KAL•uhn•dur) a chart that shows the days, weeks, and months of a year

century (SEN•chuh•ree) a period of 100 years

decade (DEK•ade) a period of ten years

month (muhnth) each of the 12 periods that make up a year (like January and December); a month lasts about 30 days

week (week) a period of seven days (Monday, Tuesday, Wednesday, Thursday, Friday, Saturday, and Sunday)

year (yeer) the time it takes Earth to make one full trip around the Sun; about 365 days

Instant Content Area Vocabulary Packets © 2011 by Joan Novelli & Holly Grundon, Scholastic Teaching Resources

Name: _____   Date: _____

Vocabulary Comics

Turtle Time

Complete the sentences in the comic strip. Use the Word Bank for help. Then read the comics!

Word Bank

calendar	month
century	week
decade	year

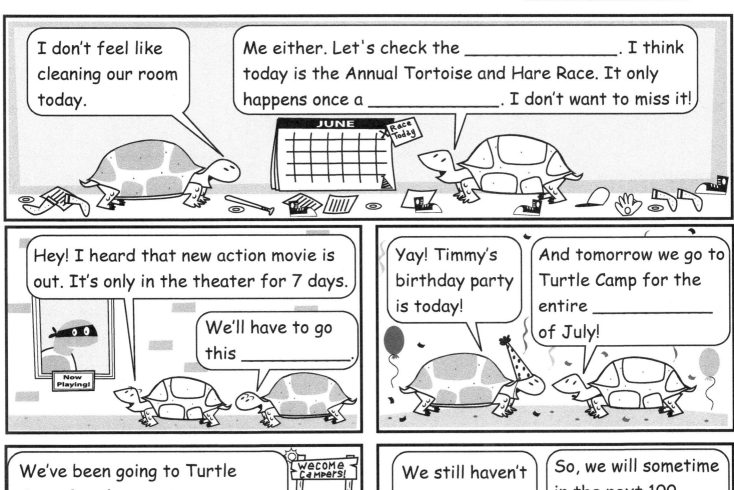

I don't feel like cleaning our room today.

Me either. Let's check the _____. I think today is the Annual Tortoise and Hare Race. It only happens once a _____. I don't want to miss it!

Hey! I heard that new action movie is out. It's only in the theater for 7 days.

We'll have to go this _____.

Yay! Timmy's birthday party is today!

And tomorrow we go to Turtle Camp for the entire _____ of July!

We've been going to Turtle Camp for almost ten years. That's nearly a _____.

We still haven't cleaned our room!

So, we will sometime in the next 100 years. You know tortoises like us can live for more than a _____!

Name: _____   Date: _____

Word Bank

- calendar
- century
- decade
- month
- week
- year

Syllable Smarties

Read each word in the Word Bank. Count the syllables. Write the words that have 1 syllable and 3 syllables.

Word Hound

Read each clue. Track down the answer! Use the Word Bank.

1. Without the first letter, this word spells **ear**: _____

2. The first four letters of this word spell **cent**: _____

3. This word and **weak** are homophones: _____

4. This word ends with a silent **e**: _____

Make a Connection

Look at a **calendar** in your classroom. Put a ✔ next to each period of time that the calendar shows you. Write a new calendar word on the last line.

_____ century   _____ month   _____ year

_____ decade   _____ week   _____

Name: _____ Date: _____

CROSSWORD

Read each clue. Write the answer in the puzzle. Fill in each box.

Across

1. 100 years or 10 decades
3. _____ days in a week
4. 10 years

Down

1. a chart that shows the days, weeks, and months
2. 12 months equal one _____
5. the fourth month in a year

Fun Fact Puzzler

Crack the code to learn a fun fact.
First find each shape in the crossword puzzle.
Then write that letter on the line above the shape.

It's equal to 1,000 years!

What is the word for 10 centuries?

m ___ ___ ___ ___ ___ ___ ___ m
   ●   ▲   ▲   ⬠   ◆   ◆   ●   ★

Name: _____ Date: _____

What do you know about multiplication and division? When you multiply, you increase a quantity by a certain number of times. To divide, you break a quantity into a certain number of parts. Look at each word below. Put a ✔ in the box that shows how much you know about that word.

Words to Know

Words	I Know That Word!	It Sounds Familiar...	It's New to Me.
divisor			
factor			
multiple			
product			
quotient			
remainder			

Word Alert! The letter **q** is almost always followed by **u**. Knowing about spelling patterns like this can help you read and spell new words.

1. Look at Words to Know.
   Write the word that begins with **qu**.

   _____

2. Use **qu** to complete each word.
   Read the words.

   _____ ick   s _____ are

   _____ iet   e _____ al

Name: _____   Date: _____

My Mini-Dictionary

Read each word and its meaning. Write a hint or draw a picture to help you learn the word.

divisor (di•VYE•zur) this number is divided into another number; the divisor comes after the ÷ in a division problem

factor (fak•tur) one of the numbers that is multiplied in a multiplication problem

multiple (MUHL•tuh•puhl) a number that can be divided evenly by another number; 25 is a multiple of 5 (so are 15 and 20)

product (PROD•uhkt) the answer in a multiplication problem

quotient (KWOH•shuhnt) the answer in a division problem

remainder (ri•MAYN•dur) the number that is left over when a number can't be exactly divided by another number

Name: _____   Date: _____

Math Mastermind II

Complete the sentences in the comic strip. Use the Word Bank for help. Then read the comics!

Word Bank

divisor	product
factor	quotient
multiple	remainder

Welcome to Math Mastermind! Today's contestants will answer questions about multiplication and division.

For 50 points, here's the first clue.

$5 \times 8 = 40$

What is a _____ ?

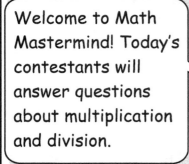

Right! For 100 points...

$3 \times 2 = 6$

What is the _____ ?

Yes! And for 200 . . .

40 is a **?** of 10.

What is _____ ?

Now for 300 . . .

$8 \div 2 = 4$

What is the _____ ?

For 400, the last clue . . .

$10 \div 2 = 5$

What is the _____ ?

And there's no _____ !

Name: _____ Date: _____

Word Bank

- divisor
- factor
- multiple
- product
- quotient
- remainder

Syllable Smarties

Read each word in the Word Bank. Count the syllables. Write the words that have 2 syllables and 3 syllables.

Word Hound

Read each clue. Track down the answer! Use the Word Bank.

1. This word has **e**, **i**, **o**, and **u** but no **a**: _____

2. This word has the little word **main** in it: _____

3. This word has a short **i** and a long **i**: _____

4. This word rhymes with **tractor**: _____

Make a Connection

How much will five pieces of candy cost? Add and then multiply to find out. Then answer the question.

○ 3¢

Add: 3 + 3 + 3 + 3 + 3 = _____   Multiply: 3 x 5 = _____

Which way is quicker? _____

Name: _____ Date: _____

CROSSWORD

Read each clue. Write the answer in the puzzle. Fill in each box.

Across

2. in 7 x 9 = 63, you _____ to find the answer

3. in 3 x 4 = 12, 4 is a _____ (so is 3!)

5. the answer in a division problem

Down

1. in 15 ÷ 3 = 5, the number 3 is the _____

2. 12 is a _____ of 2, 4, and 6

4. 10 ÷ 3 = 3, with a _____ of 1

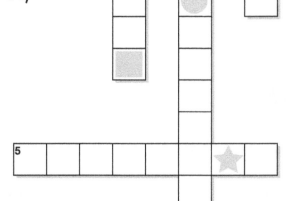

Fun Fact Puzzler

The quotient of 15 ÷ 3 is 5.

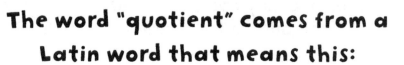

Crack the code to learn a fun fact.
First find each shape in the crossword puzzle.
Then write that letter on the line above the shape.

**The word "quotient" comes from a
Latin word that means this:**

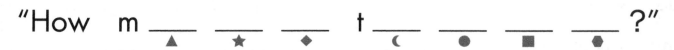

"How m __ __ __ t __ __ __ __ ?"
     ▲ ★ ◆   ☾ ● ■ ⬡

Name: _____ Date: _____

What do you know about fractions? A fraction is part of a whole. If you split a pizza equally with a friend, you each have $\frac{1}{2}$ of the whole pizza. Look at each word below. Put a ✔ in the box that shows how much you know about that word.

Words to Know

Words	I Know That Word!	It Sounds Familiar...	It's New to Me.
denominator			
equivalent			
fraction bar			
mixed number			
numerator			
simplify			

Word Alert!

Looking for familiar word parts can help you figure out new words.

Look at each word in the chart. Circle the word part that reminds you of a word you know. Write that word in the box on the right.

Word	Reminds Me of This Word
(equi)valent	equal
numerator	
simplify	

Name: _____ Date: _____

My Mini-Dictionary

Read each word and its meaning. Write a hint or draw a picture to help you learn the word.

denominator (di•NOM•uh•nay•tur) the number of equal parts into which a whole is divided; the number below the bar in a fraction

equivalent (i•KWIV•uh•luhnt) having the same value; being equal; $\frac{1}{2}$ and $\frac{2}{4}$ are equivalent fractions

fraction (FRAK•shuhn) **bar** the line between the top number and the bottom number in a fraction

mixed (mikst) **number** a number written as a whole number and a fraction; $4\frac{1}{2}$ is a mixed number

numerator (NOO•muh•ray•tur) the number above the bar in a fraction; the number of parts to be taken from the *denominator* (see above)

simplify (SIM•pluh•fye) to reduce a fraction to the lowest numbers possible (both the top and bottom numbers)

Name: _____ Date: _____

 **My Day in Fractions**

Complete the sentences in the comic strip. Use the Word Bank for help. Then read the comics!

Word Bank

denominator   mixed
equivalent   numerator
fraction bar

How was your day?

Yum!

Great! Alex gave me $\frac{1}{2}$ of his candy bar!

The top number of a fraction is the _____.

Did you have fun at recess?

Wow!

I made it $\frac{3}{4}$ of the way across the monkey bars!

Do you have much homework?

Super!

I've done $\frac{2}{3}$ of my math already!

 **3/4** The bottom number of a fraction is the _____.

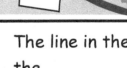 **2/3** The line in the middle is the _____ _____.

How's your report coming?

Great!

I've already written 1 $\frac{1}{2}$ pages!

For my snack, can I have $\frac{1}{2}$ of a PBJ?

Hmmmm. How about $\frac{2}{4}$?

 1 $\frac{1}{2}$ is a _____ number.

 $\frac{1}{2}$ and $\frac{2}{4}$ are the same. They are _____ fractions.

Name: _____ Date: _____

Word Bank

- denominator
- equivalent
- fraction
- mixed
- numerator
- simplify

Syllable Smarties Read each word in the Word Bank. Count the syllables. Write the words that have 2 syllables and 5 syllables.

Word Hound

Read each clue. Track down the answer! Use the Word Bank.

1. Fill in the missing letters: s ___ mpl ___ f ___

2. This word has the **kw** sound in it: _____

3. This word contains the little words **in** and **or**: _____

4. This word has **a**, **e**, **o**, and **u** but no **i**: _____

Make a Connection

If four friends divide a pizza equally, they each get $\frac{1}{4}$ of the pizza. Write about a way you use fractions in real life.

_____

_____

Name: _____   Date: _____

CROSSWORD

Read each clue. Write the answer in the puzzle. Fill in each box.

Across

2. the number below the fraction bar

5. to reduce a fraction to the lowest form

6. the number above the fraction bar

Down

1. $\frac{3}{4}$ is a _____

3. $\frac{1}{2}$ and $\frac{2}{4}$ are _____ fractions

4. $5\frac{1}{2}$ is a _____ number

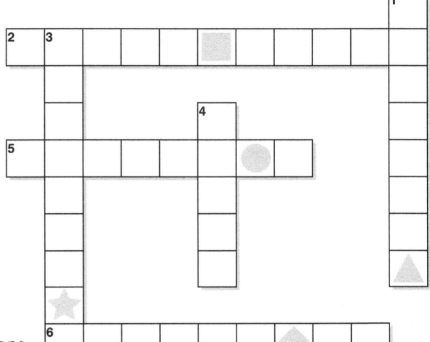

Fun Fact Puzzler

Crack the code to learn a fun fact.
First find each shape in the crossword puzzle.
Then write that letter on the line above the shape.

What is $\frac{1}{4}$ of an hour?

___ ___ ___ ___ ___ ___ ___ minutes
●   ■   ●   ◆   ★   ★   ▲

Name: _____ Date: _____

What do you know about geometry? Geometry is the study of shapes. 2-D shapes are flat. 3-D shapes look real. They have height, width, and depth. Look at each word below. Put a ✔ in the box that shows how much you know about that word.

Words to Know

Words	I Know That Word!	It Sounds Familiar...	It's New to Me.
cone			
cube			
cylinder			
prism			
pyramid			
sphere			

Word Alert! Some letters stand for more than one sound. Knowing the different sounds that letters stand for helps you read and spell words.

The **s** in **prism** has the sound of **z** in **zebra**. Write more words that have an **s** that sounds like a **z**.

 1. _____

 2. _____

 3. _____

 4. _____

Instant Content Area Vocabulary Packets © 2011 by Joan Novelli & Holly Grundon, Scholastic Teaching Resources

Name: _____ Date: _____

My Mini-Dictionary

Read each word and its meaning. Write a hint or draw a picture to help you learn the word.

cone (kone) a 3-D shape that has a round base at one end and a point at the other end

cube (kyoob) a 3-D shape that has six square sides that are the same size

cylinder (SIL•uhn•dur) a 3-D shape that is like a can; both ends of this curved shape are circles

prism (PRIZ•uhm) a *rectangular prism* has six faces that are rectangles

pyramid (PIHR•uh•mid) a 3-D shape with triangular sides that meet at a point; the base can have four sides or three sides

sphere (sfeer) a round 3-D shape that is like a ball

Name: _____   Date: _____

Vocabulary Comics

I Spy

Complete the sentences in the comic strip. Use the Word Bank for help. Then read the comics!

Word Bank

cone	prism
cube	pyramid
cylinder	sphere

I spy with my little eye something in the shape of a _____.

A paint can!

My turn. I spy with my little eye a _____.

The ball!

I spy with my little eye something shaped like a _____. It has a delicious treat inside.

The box! Some peanuts sure would be tasty.

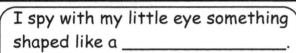

I spy with my little eye a king! And he's holding a _____!

I spy with my little eye a very good place to stop.

Ice Cream and Fudge

Mmmm . . . fudge. That's a rectangular _____.

I spy another 3-D shape, and it's in your hand!

It's my ice cream _____!

Name: _____ Date: _____

Word Bank

- cone
- cube
- cylinder
- prism
- pyramid
- sphere

Syllable Smarties

Read each word in the Word Bank. Count the syllables. Write the words that have 1 syllable and 3 syllables.

Word Hound

Read each clue. Track down the answer! Use the Word Bank.

1. This word rhymes with **phone**: _____

2. The last four letters of this word spell **here**: _____

3. Replace the **c** in this word with **t** to make **tube**: _____

4. Fill in the missing letters: p ___ r ___ m ___ d

Make a Connection

Think of something in real life that has the shape of a **cube** or **cone**. Draw a picture of it. Then fill in the sentence.

This has a _____ shape.

Name: _____   Date: _____

CROSSWORD

Read each clue. Write the answer in the puzzle. Fill in each box.

Across

2. has triangular sides that meet at a point

4. has a round base at one end and a point at the other

5. a box with six same-sized squares

Down

1. is round, like a ball

3. a _____ prism is a shape made of six rectangles

4. the shape of a can

Fun Fact Puzzler

Crack the code to learn a fun fact.
First find each shape in the crossword puzzle.
Then write that letter on the line above the shape.

What is the name in geometry for the shape of a doughnut?

A ___ ___ ___ ___ ___ ___
   ●   ▲   ★   ▲   ☾   ◆

Name: _____ Date: _____

What do you know about measurement? Rulers, clocks, and scales are used to measure things like length, time, and weight. Look at each word below. Put a ✔ in the box that shows how much you know about that word.

Words to Know

Words	I Know That Word!	It Sounds Familiar...	It's New to Me.
area			
length			
temperature			
time			
volume			
weight			

Word Alert!

Homophones are words that sound the same but have different meanings and spellings. The spelling of a homophone helps you know the correct meaning.

Look at Words to Know. Find the missing homophone. Write it on the chart. Think of a new homophone pair. Add the words to the chart.

Homophones			
for	→ four	wait	→
some	→ sum		→

Name: _____ Date: _____

My Mini-Dictionary

Read each word and its meaning. Write a hint or draw a picture to help you learn the word.

area (AIR•ee•uh) the size of a surface measured in square units

length (lengkth) the measurement of something from end to end; distance

temperature (TEM•pur•uh•chur) how hot or cold something is; temperature is measured in degrees

time (time) past, present, and future; measured in seconds, minutes, hours, days, weeks, months, and years

volume (VOL•yuhm) the volume of something in a container; measured in ounces, pints, quarts, gallons, and liters

weight (wate) how heavy or light something is; measured in ounces, pounds, and grams

Instant Content Area Vocabulary Packets © 2011 by Joan Novelli & Holly Grundon, Scholastic Teaching Resources

Name: _____   Date: _____

Vocabulary Comics

Three Pigs Build a House

Complete the sentences in the comic strip. Use the Word Bank for help. Then read the comics!

Word Bank

area	time
length	volume
temperature	weight

How many bricks do we need for this side? (We know better than to use straw or sticks!)

To find out, we need to measure the entire _____ of the wall.

Where does the _____ go? It's already 12:30. Let's break for lunch.

Grrr

We'll need a sturdy fence.

Each section will be 8 feet in _____. And it will be 6 feet high to keep out you know who!

What's the _____? It must be at least 100°F!

Soon, we can cool off in our new tub.

The _____ of this tub must be a ton or more.

It might! We got the jumbo size! Our new tub will hold a total _____ of 500 liters!

Hello, neighbors! Can I give you a hand?

Name: _____ Date: _____

Word Bank

- area
- length
- temperature
- time
- volume
- weight

Syllable Smarties

Read each word in the Word Bank. Count the syllables. Write the words that have 1 syllable and 3 syllables.

Word Hound

Read each clue. Track down the answer! Use the Word Bank.

1. This word rhymes with **dime**: _____

2. Three of the four letters in this word are vowels: _____

3. This word minus **w** spells **eight**: _____

4. The last four letters of this word are consonants: _____

Make a Connection

Many people measure things in their jobs. Look at the jobs. Tell how each person might use measurements. Write about one more person who uses measurements.

Baker: _____

Builder: _____

_____ : _____

Name: _____ Date: _____

CROSSWORD

Read each clue. Write the answer in the puzzle. Fill in each box.

Across

2. how heavy something is
4. clocks measure this
5. a farmer measures length and width to find the _____ of a field
6. a gallon of milk is a measure of _____

Down

1. the distance from one end to the other
3. how hot or cold something is

Fun Fact Puzzler

Crack the code to learn a fun fact.
First find each shape in the crossword puzzle.
Then write that letter on the line above the shape.

FEBRUARY

SUN	MON	TUE	WED	THU	FRI	SAT
					1	2
3	4	5	6	7	8	9
10	11	12	13	14	15	16
17	18	19	20	21	22	23
24	25	26	27	28	29	

Every four years, February has 29 days instead of 28! What do you call the year in which this happens?

A l __ __ __ y __ __ __
    ●   ■   ★   ●   ■   ▲

Name: _____   Date: _____

What do you know about data analysis? People collect information (data) and study it to learn more (analysis). Look at each word below. Put a ✔ in the box that shows how much you know about that word.

Words to Know

Words	I Know That Word!	It Sounds Familiar...	It's New to Me.
axis			
data			
graph			
range			
scale			
survey			

Word Alert! When the letters **ph** are together in a word, they can stand for the same sound as the letter **f**. Knowing about spelling patterns like this can help you read and spell new words.

Use the letters **ph** to complete each word. Read the words.

 1. gra _____

 2. _____ one

 3. _____ oto

 4. ele _____ ant

Name: _____   Date: _____

My Mini-Dictionary

Read each word and its meaning. Write a hint or draw a picture to help you learn the word.

axis (AK•sis) part of a graph; the x-axis is a horizontal line (goes across); the y-axis is a vertical line (goes up and down)

data (DAY•tuh) information that is collected to help answer a question

graph (graf) a chart that you can record data on; data on a bar graph is shown with horizontal or vertical bars

range (ranje) the difference between the highest number and lowest number in a set of data

scale (skale) the numbers along the axis of a graph; the scale is used to count or measure data

survey (SUR•vay) a way to collect information about a topic; many surveys include questions that are used to gather data

Name: _____   Date: _____

Mr. Moo Takes a Survey

Complete the sentences in the comic strip. Use the Word Bank for help. Then read the comics!

Word Bank

data	scale
graph	survey
range	

Mr. Moo is taking a _____. He's asking his customers: "Which new ice cream flavor do you prefer?"

Mr. Moo is making a bar _____ to represent the information.

Mr. Moo has a lot of _____ to organize!

The numbers on the _____ tell Mr. Moo how many people voted for each flavor.

Awww! My favorite, Peaches and Pickles, only got 5 votes.

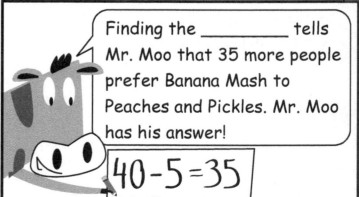

Finding the _____ tells Mr. Moo that 35 more people prefer Banana Mash to Peaches and Pickles. Mr. Moo has his answer!

$40 - 5 = 35$

Name: _____ Date: _____

Word Bank

- axis
- data
- graph
- range
- scale
- survey

Read each word in the Word Bank. Count the syllables. Write the words that have 1 syllable and 2 syllables.

Word Hound

Read each clue. Track down the answer! Use the Word Bank.

1. This word rhymes with **whale**: _____

2. This word ends in the sound of the letter **f**: _____

3. The first three letters of this word spell **ran**: _____

4. This word has the little word **at** in it: _____

Make a Connection

Mr. Moo took a **survey**. What kind of survey could you take in your classroom? Write the question you would ask.

My Survey Question: _____

_____

Name: _____   Date: _____

CROSSWORD

Read each clue. Write the answer in the puzzle. Fill in each box.

Across

3. _____ along an axis make up the scale of a graph

5. kinds of graphs: line, pie, and _____

6. subtract the lowest number from the highest number to find the _____

Down

1. data is _____ that is collected

2. the *y*-axis is a _____ line

4. take a _____ to find out everyone's favorite color

Fun Fact Puzzler

Crack the code to learn a fun fact.
First find each shape in the crossword puzzle.
Then write that letter on the line above the shape.

What is your favorite season?

What do you call a person who takes a survey?

A ___ ___ ___ ___ ___ ___ ___ ___
   ●   ■   ◆   ☾   ▲   ★   ⬡   ◆